# THE THEFT OF THE IRISH CROWN JEWELS

Argonaut Papers

First published by HMSO in 1908 as Report of the
Viceregal Commission Appointed to Investigate the
Circumstances of the Loss of the Regalia of the Order of
Saint Patrick (Cd 3906). © Crown copyright .This selection
and this edition © Tim Coates.

A CIP catalogue record for this book is available from the
British Library.

Argonaut Papers

ISBN: 978-1-84381-040-7

Editor: Frances Maher

Keying: Tricia Lord

Series Design: David C

'The repackaging of classics is a tried and trusted winner, but Tim Coates has come up with something entirely original: the repackaging of history. He has transformed papers [from archives] ... into verbatim narratives, so, for instance, in UFOs in the House of Lords we get a hilarious recreation, directly from Hansard, of a nutty debate that took place in 1979 ... This is inspired publishing, not only archivally valuable but capable of bringing the past back to life without the usual filter of academic or biographer.' Guardian

'It is difficult to praise the idea, the format, the selection and the quality of the series too highly.' Times Higher Education Supplement

'Who, outside a few historians, knows that the British invaded Tibet? We approach these stories with an immediacy it would be impossible to contrive ... from one of the richest unexplored attics in the country.' Robert Winder, The Independent

'This is raw history ... An excellent series. It's particularly satisfying to see Goering getting a dressing down from a British diplomat.' [on Dealing with Hitler] Military Illustrated

'Very good to read … insight into important things … inexorably moving … If you want to read about the Titanic, you won't read a better thing … a revelation.' (on The Loss of The Titanic) Open Book, BBC Radio 4

'The account is humane, moving and beautifully told. Each pocket size edition tells a good story. This excellent series makes enjoyable reading. More please.' [on Tragedy at Bethnal Green] Times Higher Education Supplement

'Congratulations … for unearthing and reissuing such an enjoyable vignette.'[on Wilfred Blunt's Egyptian Garden] The Spectator

# THE THEFT OF THE IRISH CROWN JEWELS

*The Unsolved Mystery, 1907*

Series editor: Tim Coates

Argonaut Papers

Tim Coates studied at University College, Oxford and at the University of Stirling. After working in the theatre for a number of years, he took up bookselling and became managing director, firstly of Sherratt and Hughes bookshops, and then of Waterstone's. He is known for his support for foreign literature, particularly from the Czech Republic, and specializes in the republishing of interesting archives. He also actively seeks improvement in the public library service.

The idea for this series came while searching through the bookshelves of his late father-in-law, Air Commodore Patrick Cave OBE. Tim Coates is married to Bridget Cave, has two sons and lives in London. He is the author of *Patsy: The Story of Mary Cornwallis West,* published by Bloomsbury in 2003 and *Aldeburgh, a portrait,* published by Antique Collectors' Club, in 2009.

Tim Coates welcomes views and ideas on the series.

He can be e-mailed at tim.coates@yahoo.com.

*The 'Irish Crown Jewels' – the regalia or insignia of the Order of St Patrick, a chivalric order founded by the government in 1783 – mysteriously disappeared on or before 6th July 1907, as King Edward VII was on the point of visiting Ireland to invest a knight of the Order of St Patrick.*

*The Press commentary in the months following the robbery included speculation about where the jewels might be and how they might be found, even by mystic intervention. The relationships between the various parties and the possibility of the depraved nature of social life in Dublin Castle became an open house.*

*However, the task entrusted to the Vice-Regal Commission appointed by the Lord Lieutenant-General and General Governor of Ireland was not to conduct a criminal investigation but to determine whether Sir Arthur Vicars, the Ulster King of Arms (the state heraldic and genealogical officer in charge of the Office of Arms in Dublin Castle) had 'exercised due vigilance and proper care' as the custodian of the star and badge.*

*The report, with its extraordinary revelations, of the Vice-Regal Commission and Sir Arthur Vicars' statements to the police are reproduced here in full.*

*In order to avoid repetition, the Minutes of Evidence have been abbreviated, and the evidence of some of the minor witnesses has been excluded if adequately covered elsewhere.*

*Note: the purchasing value of £1 in 1900 was about 100 times the value of £1 in 2000. Therefore a loan of £100 at the time of The Theft of the Crown Jewels would now be worth £10,000 and a loan of £750 would now be worth £75,000.*

And it is ordained that, in pursuance of the Royal Ordinance of Our Royal Predecessor, King William the Fourth, bearing date the seventh day of March, one thousand eight hundred and thirty-one, the jewelled Insignia of the Grand Master made by Command of His said late Majesty for the use of the Grand Master of the said Most Illustrious Order, of which a description and representation is hereunto annexed, and which are Crown Jewels, shall be handed over by each Lord Lieutenant-General and General Governor of Ireland, Grand Master of the said Most Illustrious Order, to his successor at such time as the Sword of State, is delivered over, and shall be deposited by Our Ulster King of Arms in the Chancery of the Order along with the other Insignia of the Order.

- A Large Star composed of fine Brilliant Rays and Circles with Emerald Shamrock on a Ruby Cross; in the centre the Motto of the Order *(Quis separabit?* – Who shall separate?) in Diamonds on blue enamelled ground.

- A Large Badge of the Order of Saint Patrick, pendent from a representation of a Harp ensigned with the Imperial Crown, all composed of fine Brilliants with Emerald Shamrock on a Ruby Cross; in the centre the Motto of the Order in Diamonds on blue enamelled ground, surrounded by a Wreath of Shamrocks in Emeralds, the whole enclosed by a Circle surmounted by the Harp and Crown in Brilliants.

- A Gold Badge of the Order of Saint Patrick, pendent from a representation of a Harp ensigned with the Imperial Crown richly enamelled and jewelled with Emeralds and Rubies.

\-        It is ordained that on the decease of each and every Knight Companion of this Most Illustrious Order, the heirs, executors and administrators of all such Knights Companions shall, within three months after the decease of any such Knight, deliver the before-mentioned Collars and Badges to the Sovereign or the Grand Master, for the service of the Order. And Ulster King of Arms, or his Deputy, shall have full power in the name of the Grand Master to apply to the heirs, executors or administrators of such deceased Knights for the Collars and Badges aforesaid.

\-        And it is further ordained that the said Collars and Badges shall be deposited for safe keeping in a steel safe in the strongroom in the Chancery of the Order in the Office of Arms in Ireland until they be disposed of by the Grand Master. And when the said Badges and Collars are delivered to any Knight by order of the Grand Master, he shall give a receipt for the same to Ulster King of Arms, or to his Deputy.

\-        It is ordained that Our Ulster King of Arms for the time being shall be the King of Arms, Knight Attendant on the Order, and shall have the custody of the Seal and of the Archives of the Order and the jewelled Insignia of the Grand Master. He shall attend to the service of the Order generally, and shall obey and execute such commands and directions as he may receive from the Sovereign or the Grand Master relating to the same.

- We are further pleased to ordain that the Chancery
of the said Most Illustrious Order, wherein a
record of all proceedings connected therewith shall
be carefully deposited and preserved, shall be in
the Office of Arms in Our Castle of Dublin.

*Extracts from the Statutes of the Order of St Patrick, passed
under the Royal Sign Manual on 29th July 1905*

Warrant Appointing the Vice-Regal Commission

By the Lord Lieutenant-General and General Governor of Ireland

Whereas We have deemed it expedient that a Commission should issue forthwith to investigate the circumstances of the loss of the Regalia of the Order of Saint Patrick and to inquire whether Sir Arthur Vicars exercised due vigilance and proper care as the custodian thereof.

Now We, John Campbell, Earl of Aberdeen, Lord Lieutenant-General and General Governor of Ireland, nominate, constitute and appoint you, His Honor James Johnston Shaw, Robert Fitzwilliam Starkie, Esquire, and Chester Jones, Esquire, to be Commissioners for the purposes of the said inquiry.

We do by these presents authorize and empower you to inquire of and concerning the premises, and to examine witnesses, and call for and examine all such books and documents as you shall judge likely to afford you the fullest information, and to report to Us what you shall find touching and concerning the premises.

Given at His Majesty's Castle in Dublin, this 6th day of January 1908. By His Excellency's Command.

J. B.Dougherty

Contents

Witnesses

Mr Alexander Loftus Bond

Chief Inspector Richard Cummins

Mr Cornelius Gallagher

Mr Francis Bennett Goldney twice

Mr W.V. Harrel thrice

Mr John Crawford Hodgson

Sir George C.V. Holmes Chief Inspector

John Kane twice

Detective Officer Owen Kerr twice

Superintendent John Lowe

Mr Peirce Gun Mahony

Detective-Sergeant Patrick Murphy

Mr F.J. O'Hare

Colonel Sir John Ross of Bladensburg,

KCB Mr Francis Richard Shackleton

Detective-Sergeant Sheehan

To His Excellency The Lord Lieutenant-General and General Governor of Ireland

May it please your excellence

We, the undersigned, were, by Your Excellency's Warrant bearing date the 6th day of January 1908 appointed Commissioners to inquire into and report upon 'the circumstances of the loss of the Regalia of the Order of St Patrick' and to inquire whether Sir Arthur Vicars exercised 'due vigilance and proper care as the custodian thereof '. And we now beg to report to Your Excellency as follows:

We held our first meeting on 10th January 1908 at the Office of Arms, Dublin Castle. The Right Hon. J.H. Campbell, KC, MP, and Mr Timothy M. Healy, KC, MP (instructed by Messrs W.R. Meredith and Son, Solicitors) appeared as counsel on behalf of Sir Arthur Vicars; the Solicitor-General for Ireland, Mr Redmond Barry, KC, MP (instructed by Mr Malachi Kelly, Chief Crown Solicitor) appeared on behalf of the government.

At the outset of our proceedings Mr J.H. Campbell, as counsel for Sir Arthur Vicars, asked us whether the inquiry was to be public or private. We informed him that we were prepared to hear any application he had to make on that point, and to consider it carefully. He then proceeded to apply that the inquiry might be held in public. As most of his arguments were based upon the terms of the reference in Your Excellency's Warrant, and upon the absence of any power in your Commissioners to compel the attendance of witnesses or to examine them upon oath, we pointed out that these objections applied to any inquiry at all under Your Excellency's Warrant, whether public or private.

Mr Campbell then declared that under no circumstances could Sir Arthur Vicars or his counsel take any part in an inquiry held under Your Excellency's Warrant, and withdrew his application for a public inquiry. Sir Arthur Vicars and his counsel then withdrew, and we have had no assistance from them in our inquiry. We had the advantage, however, of the written statements made by Sir Arthur Vicars to the police and of the oral statements made by him at various times to the police and other witnesses examined before us.

On the withdrawal of Sir Arthur Vicars we adjourned till the next morning, in order that we might consider, and give the government time to consider, the situation that had thus arisen. We were disposed to think that no useful purpose could be served by the prosecution of the inquiry after the withdrawal of Sir Arthur Vicars, who, as the responsible custodian of the jewels, was the person mainly interested in the result of the inquiry; and in view of the fact that the government were probably already in possession of all the information which our inquiry was likely, under the circumstances, to elicit.

But when the Solicitor-General, on behalf of the government, asked us to hear the evidence relevant to our inquiry which he was in a position to offer, and assured us he was in possession of important evidence on both branches of our inquiry, we felt that we could not refuse to receive and record the evidence thus tendered, and that we must leave the responsibility for any deficiencies in the evidence before us on those who refused to take part in our proceedings.

We took evidence on five days, January 11, 13, 14, 15 and 16, and during that time there were examined before us every person employed in the Office of Arms during the year 1907, except Sir Arthur Vicars himself, Mr Horlock, his clerk, and Miss Gibbon, the typist. We sat in the Library of the Office of

Arms where the safe containing the lost jewels stood at the time of the robbery, and we had a full opportunity of inspecting, on the spot, all the arrangements of the office.

We also examined every police officer who had been engaged in the investigation of the circumstances attending the robbery, and certain experts in the construction and use of safes and safe-locks, who gave us valuable information. We have thus been able to ascertain every material circumstance connected with the loss of the Crown Jewels, and we propose to give Your Excellency, in the first place, a short statement of the facts which appear to us to be the most important in relation to the subject of our inquiry.

Sir Arthur Vicars was appointed Ulster King of Arms in February 1893. At that time the Office of Arms was in the Bermingham Tower, but in 1903 it was removed to the building now occupied in the Upper Castle Yard. The duties of Ulster King of Arms in relation to the custody of the Crown Jewels and of the other insignia of the Order of St Patrick are defined in the revised Statutes of the Order, dated 29 July 1905.

By Statute 27, Ulster King of Arms 'shall have the custody of the … jewelled insignia of the Grand Master'. By Statute 12, 'the jewelled insignia of the Grand Master … which are Crown Jewels … shall be deposited by our Ulster King of Arms in the Chancery of the Order, along with the other Insignia of the Order'. By Statute 37, the Chancery of the Order 'shall be in the Office of Arms in Our Castle of Dublin'. And by Statute 20 it is ordained that the collars and badges of the Knights Companions of the Order which are in the custody of Ulster King of Arms 'shall be deposited for safe keeping in a steel safe in the strongroom+ in the Chancery of the Order in the Office of Arms in Ireland'.

At the fitting up of the new Office of Arms in 1903 a strongroom was built by the Board of Works according to plans approved by Sir Arthur Vicars. Sir George Holmes, the chairman of the Board of Works, informed us that, at the time the plans for this strongroom were prepared, he was not told by Sir Arthur Vicars, nor did he know, that the safe in which the Crown Jewels and other insignia were kept was to be placed in the strongroom. After the strongroom was completed it was found that the safe could not be got in by the door. When Sir George Holmes's attention was called to this, he offered to place the safe in the strongroom either by breaking down part of the wall and rebuilding it or by temporarily removing the iron bars of the window.

Sir Arthur Vicars did not accept this offer on the ground that the safe would occupy too much floor space in the strongroom and said that unless he got a smaller safe he would prefer it to remain outside. It was ultimately arranged that the safe should remain in the Library until it was wanted for some other office, when Sir George Holmes promised to provide a new safe which could be placed in the strongroom. According to the evidence of Sir George Holmes this arrangement was acquiesced in by Sir Arthur Vicars, and so matters remained down to the date of the disappearance of the jewels.

Sir George Holmes told us that his attention was never called by Sir Arthur Vicars, or anybody else, after July 1905, to the requirements of Statutes 12 and 20, that the Crown Jewels and other insignia of the Order of St Patrick 'shall be deposited for safe keeping in a steel safe in the strongroom'. It is certain that this requirement of the Statutes was never complied with and that from the date of entering upon the new office in 1903 until the date of the disappearance of the jewels, the safe was kept, not in the strongroom, but in the Library.

The Office of Arms is entered by an outer door opening into the Upper Castle Yard. There are two locks on that door, a latch opened by a latchkey and a large stock-lock with a keyhole both inside and outside, the stock or main lock was never locked by day or night. The door was shut at night and on Sundays and holidays by slipping the bolt of the latch, so that any person having a latchkey could enter at any time of the day or night when the office was closed. When the latch was unlocked the door was opened by turning a handle. There was no bell on the door to indicate when it was being opened or shut.

There were at least seven latchkeys for this door outstanding. Sir Arthur Vicars, Mr Burtchaell, Secretary, Mr P.G. Mahony, Cork Herald, William Stivey, the messenger, Mrs Farrell, the office cleaner, Detective Kerr and John O'Keeffe, a servant of the Board of Works, each had a latchkey. It was necessary that Mrs Farrell, Stivey, Detective Kerr and O'Keeffe (who lit and extinguished the light in the Clock Tower during the Castle season) should have access to the office at times when it was closed, and perhaps no better arrangement could conveniently have been made. But it is obvious that the fact that the office was so easily accessible at all hours and that seven latchkeys were given out, some of them in the hands of persons of humble station, made it additionally necessary that special provision should be made for the safe keeping of the Crown Jewels.

During the day this outer door could be opened by anybody merely by turning the handle. There was no one on the ground floor but the messenger Stivey, whose usual seat did not command a view of the door. The Library, in which the safe containing the Crown Jewels was kept, is not an ordinary working room and is not occupied, except temporarily, by any of the officials. One door of the Library is quite close to the outer door, and is so situated that any person might quietly open the outer door and enter the Library without attracting attention. A second door of the Library opened into the messenger's room and was usually left open.

The Library was the waiting-room of the office, and every person who called on a matter of business or curiosity was shown in there until some of the officials came down from the first floor to attend to him. The Office of Arms, in common with all the other offices in Dublin Castle, was visited and inspected every evening, after all the officials had left, by a member of the detective force, whose duty it was to see that the offices were safe, but who had no special duty in connection with the custody of the Crown Jewels.

The strongroom is practically an offshoot from the messenger's room in which Stivey sat when on duty except when he was sent on a message, or was at dinner or was called upstairs. There were four keys for the outer door of this strongroom. One was in possession of Sir Arthur Vicars, Stivey held one, Mr P.G. Mahony one, and one, which had for a short time been in possession of Mr Burtchaell, was, at the date of the disappearance of the jewels, in the strongroom in a drawer stated to be unlocked.

Close inside the outer door of the strongroom is a strong steel grille which must be opened before access can be had to the strongroom. One key of this grille, which was in Stivey's charge, was constantly in the lock whether the strongroom was open or shut, except when Stivey went on a message or was at dinner, when he locked the grille and placed the key of the grille in an unlocked drawer in his room, leaving the outer door of the strongroom open. This latter arrangement was made by Sir Arthur Vicars' order. Every official in the office knew where the key of the grille was kept in Stivey's absence, and had access to it.

It was the custom for Stivey to open the strongroom every morning when he came on duty, and to leave both the outer door and the grille open until he left in the evening, except upon occasions of his temporary absence, when he made the arrangements which we have already described. If he were merely called upstairs and there was no stranger about, he left both the outer door and the grille open.

This strong-room ought to have contained the safe in which the Crown Jewels and other insignia were kept, but it did, as a matter of fact, contain articles of very great value, including three gold collars and badges of Knights Companions of the Order, two state maces, the sword of state, a jewelled sceptre, a crown and two massive silver spurs. These were exposed in a glass case. There was another gold collar in a case somewhere else in the strongroom. It is plainly contrary to Statute 20 of the Order that these collars and badges of the Knights Companions should be kept exposed in a glass case in the strong-room. The words of the Statute are express: 'in a steel safe in the strongroom'.

We have thus given a general description of the way in which the Office of Arms was kept, and of the provision made for the safe keeping of the Crown Jewels and other insignia of the Order of St Patrick. We have stated no facts but those which are common to all the witnesses, and which are admitted by Sir Arthur Vicars himself in his statements to the police.

Looking at these facts alone, and without any reference to the loss of the Crown Jewels or the incidents that accompanied that loss, we cannot arrive at the conclusion that Sir Arthur Vicars exercised due vigilance and proper care in the custody of the jewels. We do not dwell upon the positive breaches of his duty under Statutes 12 and 20 of the Order. But, apart from any specific duty imposed upon him by the Statutes, we cannot think that he showed proper care in leaving the safe containing the Crown Jewels in a room which was open to the public all day, and was open all night to any person who either possessed or could get possession of one of seven latchkeys.

We should have thought that in the case of jewels like these, of immense value and of national importance, the responsible custodian would, instead of carrying about the key of the safe in his pocket, have deposited it with his banker or in some other place of security except on the rare occasions when it was necessarily in use. We are of opinion that great want of proper care was also shown in respect of the strongroom.

The fact that three, and at one time four, keys of this room were out in the hands of different persons, one of whom was Stivey, the messenger, who also had control of a key of the grille, is in itself a proof of want of due care. We have been unable to ascertain any sufficient reason why a key of this strongroom should have been in any hands but Sir Arthur Vicars' own. The further fact that it was the custom that William Stivey the messenger should open both doors of the strongroom on his arrival in the morning and that they should be kept open all day until Stivey left in the evening also appears to us to show great want of care.

We now come to the circumstances connected with the loss of the jewels and with the discovery of their loss. It is ascertained beyond doubt that the jewels were in the safe on 11th June 1907. They were shown on that date by Sir Arthur Vicars to Mr John Crawford Hodgson, Librarian to the Duke of Northumberland. There is no evidence that from that date until the 6th of July, when their loss was discovered, they were seen by anybody, nor is there any evidence that the safe was ever opened by anyone in the office between those dates.

Sir Arthur Vicars himself says: 'From 11th June to 6th July I have no recollection of seeing the jewels nor of having gone to the safe.' The officials attending in the office between those dates were Sir Arthur Vicars, Mr Burtchaell, Mr Mahony, Mr Horlock, Miss Gibbon, Stivey the messenger, and Mrs Farrell the office cleaner. Neither Mr Goldney, Athlone Pursuivant, nor Mr Shackleton, Dublin Herald, appears to have been in the office, or indeed in Ireland, at any time between those dates. Mr Mahony was not in the office from April until 4th July, except on one day in May, so that, of the period between 1th June and 6th July, he was only in the office on three days.

On the morning of Wednesday 3rd July Mrs Farrell, the office cleaner, on coming to the office at her usual hour between seven and eight o'clock, found that the outer door was unlocked. The bolt of the latch was caught back, so that she opened the door by merely turning the handle. Mrs Farrell waited until Stivey, the messenger, came in about 10 a.m., and told him what had happened. When Sir Arthur Vicars arrived about 12 noon, Stivey told him what Mrs Farrell had reported, and Sir Arthur replied, 'Is that so?' or 'Did she?' No further notice was taken of this incident. It was not reported to the police, nor was Kerr, the detective, whose duty it was to inspect the offices at night, informed of the circumstance. Stivey is perfectly certain that he slipped the bolt of the latch when leaving the office about 5.30 on the Tuesday evening, but he is not certain whether he left Sir Arthur Vicars behind him or not.

Detective Kerr visited the office about 7 p.m. on the Tuesday evening, opened the door by his latchkey, found it locked, found no one in the office, made his usual round of inspection, tried the door as he went out and made sure it was locked. It is plain upon this evidence that someone in possession of a latchkey visited the office after Detective Kerr had left it, and took the trouble to draw back the bolt of the latch and fasten it. It seems to us an extraordinary instance of negligence on Sir Arthur Vicars' part that he made no enquiry about this singular incident, did not interrogate Kerr the detective, made no report to the police and did not examine the safe or strong-room to see that all was right.

Sir Arthur Vicars' own account of this matter is as follows: 'On Wednesday 3rd July, to the best of my recollection, I arrived at the office at 12 noon, and left about 6 p.m. Stivey informed me that he was told by Mrs Farrell, the office cleaner, that she found the hall door open when she arrived to clean the office in the morning.'

On the morning of Saturday 6th July a still more startling incident occurred. Mrs Farrell opened the office at her usual hour between 7 and 8 a.m. and walked into the messenger's room to see if any written message had been left for her. On entering the messenger's room she found that the outer door of the strongroom was standing ajar. There were two keys hanging in the lock of the grille. Mrs Farrell took these two keys out of the grille lock and shut the outer door of the strongroom. She did not wait until Stivey came, either because he was late or because she was in a hurry, but she wrote a note on his blotting-pad telling him what she had found, and left the keys on the note.

When Stivey came about 10.20 a.m., he found Mrs Farrell's note and the two keys lying beside it. These two keys, as he explained to us, were the key of the grille and a smaller key which opened the presses in the Library, and they were tied together by a piece of twine. The presence of the keys was indubitable evidence that the strong-room door had been opened or had been left open, as the keys were left in the lock of the grille the night before. Stivey at once examined the strongroom, and found that nothing had been touched inside, so far as he could observe.

On the preceding evening Stivey had gone to Sir Arthur Vicars' room about 5.30 p.m. and found him there with Mr Horlock. He asked Sir Arthur if he might go, and was told he might. He asked Sir Arthur if he wanted the strongroom any more that night. Sir Arthur said, 'No, you may close it'. Stivey then closed and locked the outer door of the strongroom, leaving the two keys hanging in the lock of the grille. Stivey's statement is fully confirmed by Sir Arthur Vicars, who says: 'On Friday 5th July I left the office at 7.15 p.m. About 5.45 p.m. Stivey asked me whether he could go, and I said 'Yes'. He asked me whether he should lock the strongroom, and I told him to do so, at the same time handing him a manuscript to be replaced therein. I subsequently had occasion to pass the strongroom door to go to the telephone more than once, and the door was closed.'

About 7.15 p.m. Sir Arthur Vicars left his office with Mr Horlock. Before he left he made what he called his 'usual tour of inspection'. 'I passed through the Library, glancing at all the bookcases and satisfied myself they were closed. I passed into the messenger's room, noticed the window was bolted and tried the handle of the strongroom door and found the door was locked.' Almost immediately after Sir Arthur Vicars had left the office Detective Kerr entered it, and examined every room in the house. He noticed the strongroom door; it was closed and bolted. He left the office about 7.30 p.m.

On these facts it was plain that someone had entered the office after the detective had left on Friday evening, and had opened the strongroom and left it open. It seems very strange that, after what had happened on the preceding Wednesday morning, Sir Arthur Vicars should treat this new incident as if it were of no importance whatever. When he was told by Stivey that Mrs Farrell had found the strongroom open when she came in the morning, he said, 'Did she?' or 'Is that so?' went upstairs to his own room, and took no further notice of the incident. He did not even examine the strongroom to see if anything had been taken, he did not examine the safe to see if it had been tampered with, he did not send for Detective Kerr to see if he had noticed anything wrong the night before and he made no communication to the police.

Sir Arthur Vicars has given his own explanation of his conduct on this occasion, and it seems to us wholly insufficient: 'On Saturday 6th July I arrived at the office at about 11 a.m. I have a vague recollection of being told by Stivey that Mrs Farrell had found the strongroom door open when she arrived, but at the time I did not realize that it was that morning, and being very busy left the matter for subsequent investigation. It was not until Sunday afternoon, when I was working at my house in connection with the royal visit with Horlock, that I realized that the strongroom door was open on Saturday morning. Horlock had informed me at my house on Sunday that Stivey had told me in my office on Saturday that the strongroom door was found open that morning.'

It is hardly necessary to comment upon the strange want of any sense of responsibility for the security of his office and of the jewels entrusted to his care which this statement reveals. The door of his office had been found open on the previous Wednesday; he is now told that the door of the strongroom had been found open; he has only a vague recollection of this startling statement; he does not take the trouble to ascertain definitely even the day on which the event had happened; and he thinks it a matter that may be left for subsequent investigation. We can only say that, in our opinion, Sir Arthur Vicars' treatment of this incident shows an entire absence of vigilance and care in the custody of the jewels.

It was between 12.30 and 1 p.m. on Saturday 6th July that Stivey told Sir Arthur Vicars about the strongroom having been found open. About 2.15 p.m. on the same day Stivey went to Sir Arthur Vicars' room to inquire whether he might go for the day. Sir Arthur gave him the key of the safe, and the box containing the collar of a deceased knight of St Patrick which had just been returned, and told him to open the safe and place the collar in it. This was the first time that Stivey ever had the key of the safe in his hand.

It seems strange that Stivey should at any time have been entrusted with the key of the safe, but that he should have been entrusted with it just after the occurrence of incidents which called for peculiar care seems stranger still. Stivey proceeded to the safe and tried to open it. He found that the safe was actually unlocked. He did not open the safe.

Sir Arthur Vicars came downstairs immediately and Stivey told him the safe was not locked. Sir Arthur thereupon opened the safe, and found that the jewels and all the collars and badges in the safe were gone. The cases which had contained the jewels, collars and badges had all been carefully replaced, but a case containing his mother's diamonds, which was locked and the key of which was in the hands of Mr George Mahony, his half-brother, had been removed.

The police were then sent for and told what had happened, and even then not a word was said about the strong-room having been found open that very morning. When Superintendent Lowe said, 'What about the strong-room?' Sir Arthur replied: 'It is a modern safe, a Milner's safe, and quite secure; it could not be opened except by its own key.' Nobody on Saturday 6th mentioned to the police either that the outer door had been found open on the morning of Wednesday or that the strongroom had been found open on that morning

(Saturday), and it was only on Sunday 7th that Detective Kerr heard these facts from Mrs Farrell for the first time.

The lock of the strongroom was carefully examined on Monday 8th July by Mr F.J. O'Hare, a Dublin representative of the Milner Safe Company, who supplied the door and lock of the strong-room. He took the lock to pieces and took out the seven levers. He found no trace whatever of tampering with the lock. There was not a scratch on the highly polished levers. The Ratner safe, in which the jewels were kept, was examined on the 9th July by Cornelius Gallagher, an employee of Ratner's agents in Dublin. He removed the lock and chamber, took all the levers out and found no trace of tampering or any scratch on the levers.

Both these experts came to the same conclusion; that there was no picking of the locks, or attempt at picking; that the locks were opened by their own keys or keys identical with them in every respect in make and finish, and that such keys could not be fabricated from a wax impression. Keys fabricated from a wax impression, though they would have opened the locks, would, in their opinion, have left on the levers traces of pressure and friction which would be easy discernible.

If the person who stole the jewels was, as we believe he was, the same person who entered the Office of Arms on the night of Tuesday 2nd July and again on the night of Friday 5th July, it is clear that he possessed three keys - a latchkey for the outer door, a key of the strong-room and a key of the safe. As there were at least seven latchkeys outstanding and carried about in the pockets of the persons who used them there could be no great difficulty in obtaining possession of a latchkey.

Sir Arthur Vicars told Sergeant Sheehan on the 20th September that his own latchkey had been lost on the previous

28th June, and that he did not recover it until the 9th or 10th July, when it was found on his dressing table. It is evident that this latchkey of Sir Arthur Vicars, in whatever hands it was, might have been used to open the door at any time between the 28th June and 9th July.

There were four keys of the strong-room. One of these, which had for a short time been in possession of Mr Burtchaell, was, at the date of the disappearance of the jewels and for a year before, kept concealed in the strong-room. There was no evidence that this key had ever been removed from the strong-room until after the discovery of the loss of the jewels. Another key of the strongroom was in possession of Mr P.G. Mahony, Cork Herald. Stivey seemed to be under the impression that Mr Mahony's key was in the strong-room with Mr Burtchaell's, but we are satisfied, on Mr Mahony's own evidence, that his key was locked up in a desk in his own house from some day in April 1907, when he left Dublin on account of his health, until the evening of Saturday 6th July, when he delivered up this key to Sir Arthur Vicars, and that it had not been once out of his desk during that interval. There remain only Stivey's key and that held by Sir Arthur Vicars himself.

We are of opinion that the strong-room must have been opened on the night of Friday 5th July by one or other of these keys, or else by a key fabricated by a skilled workman from one of the keys of the strong-room as a model. There was no evidence that any of these keys was ever out of its holder's possession long enough to enable a false key to be made, and we had evidence from the police that an exhaustive inquiry had been made amongst all the locksmiths and key manufacturers in Dublin, and no such key had been made by any of them.

We are also of opinion, with Inspector Kane, of Scotland Yard, that it is difficult to believe that any thief would have taken the trouble and risk of getting a false key of the strong-room fabricated, except for the purpose of removing the valuables from the glass case therein. The person who opened the strong-room on the night of Friday 5th July touched nothing in it.

We cannot attribute negligence to Sir Arthur Vicars in the custody of his key of the strong-room. He seems to have taken as much care of it as any man could do of a key which he carried about with him, and which was in constant use. We have already expressed an opinion that it was an imprudent thing to give a key of the strong-room to a man in Stivey's position, though we are fully convinced of Stivey's probity. Stivey himself says that he knew of no reason for his having this key except that Sir Arthur Vicars wanted him to carry a key.

There were only two keys of the safe, both in the possession of Sir Arthur Vicars. We are of opinion, upon the evidence, that the safe could only have been opened by one of these two keys, or by a key made by a skilled workman from one of these keys as a model. The following is Sir Arthur Vicars' own account of the way in which the two keys were kept:

'So far as I know there are only two keys for the safe which are always in my custody. ... The key of the safe which I use I always carry with me along with other keys on a steel ring, except on full dress nights when I remove it from the bunch and carry it on a ring of its own in my uniform coat pocket; the other key for the safe I have always kept concealed in my residence. ... I recollect leaving the key of the safe in my writing table at my residence about two months ago, but the keys, with safe key included, were brought to me to my office by my servant, Frederick Pitt, within an hour. The keys were found by my maidservant in my writing desk, and she directed Pitt to bring them to the Castle to me. A further statement was made by Sir Arthur Vicars about the second key of the safe to Mr Harrel, Assistant Commissioner of the Dublin Metropolitan Police, on the afternoon of Saturday 6th July, the day on which the loss of the jewels was discovered: 'He told me he had a second key for the safe, and that that key was in a drawer in a writing table in his own house. I said to him: "Would you go and see whether that key is now there?" He said he had so much to do that he could not go then, but would go at the earliest moment possible - about seven o'clock. I asked him to let me know at once when he went home whether the key was there, and he said he would. And he telephoned to me that evening that the key was there just as he had left it, and that he could see no trace of it having been tampered with.'

We cannot acquit Sir Arthur Vicars of want of proper care in the custody of the keys of the safe. These keys unlocked the safe which contained jewels of enormous value and importance, for whose safety Sir Arthur Vicars was wholly responsible. The safe was placed in a room which was easily accessible by day to everybody, and by night to anybody who could get possession of a latchkey. The position and value of these jewels must have been known to very many people, as Sir Arthur Vicars was in the habit of showing them freely to casual visitors in the Library, where people were passing in and out. It was not necessary to open the safe except upon very rare occasions. Sir Arthur Vicars himself says: 'I seldom have occasion to open it.'

It appears on his own statement that he did not open the safe between 11th June and 6th July. Under these circumstances it appears to us that Sir Arthur Vicars ought not to have carried about a key of the safe or left one in his own house. He ought to have deposited the two keys of the safe in a strong room at his bankers or in some other place of equal security, and only taken out one when it was necessary to open the safe, and returned it again to its place of security as soon as the occasion for using it was over.

We have thus given Your Excellency a statement of all the essential facts and circumstances connected with the loss of the Crown Jewels and of the conclusions we have drawn from them as to the vigilance and care exercised by Sir Arthur Vicars in their custody. Your Excellency will observe that the main facts on which we base any conclusion affecting Sir Arthur Vicars are not in controversy. There has been no conflict of evidence as to these facts before us, and there is nothing to contradict them in the various statements made by Sir Arthur Vicars himself to the police.

We are very sorry that Sir Arthur Vicars did not appear before us to give evidence or to assist us, through his counsel, in the examination or cross-examination of other witnesses. We think the reasons assigned for his refusal to assist us are wholly insufficient.

Objection was at first taken to our inquiry being held in private. We were ready to hear an application for a public inquiry and to grant it, if good reason had been shown for it, but as soon as we intimated our readiness to hear such an application it was withdrawn, and the objection to our Commission based on other and wholly different grounds.

Objection was taken to the terms of the reference, though we think that the terms of the reference were wide enough to embrace every matter in relation to the loss of the Crown Jewels in which Sir Arthur Vicars' conduct as their custodian was involved.

Objection was taken to the powers of the Commission, although we possessed every power which any royal or vice-regal commission can possess without a special Act of Parliament.

The absence of power to compel the attendance of witnesses was made a matter of objection by Sir Arthur Vicars and his counsel; but the only witnesses asked by us to attend who refused to come, in addition to Sir Arthur Vicars himself, were Mr Horlock, his clerk, and Miss Gibbon, the typist, both of whom based their refusal on the ground of the supposed interest of Sir Arthur Vicars. We do not think that the administration of an oath would have affected the results of an inquiry in which there was little conflict of evidence as to the details, and in which all the salient and essential facts were agreed upon by everybody interested.

When much evidence had been given before us which seemed to us to show great want of due care and vigilance on Sir Arthur Vicars' part in the custody of the lost jewels, we thought it only fair to give him another opportunity of appearing before us and telling his own story in person. On the application of the Solicitor-General we agreed to take his evidence and that of any witnesses he might suggest, in public, if he so desired. Sir Arthur Vicars refused this offer, and we have not had the advantage of hearing from himself directly his account of the various matters and occurrences in which he was concerned.

In these circumstances it is a great satisfaction to us to be able to say that, having carefully examined and considered every statement which Sir Arthur Vicars has made either in writing or orally relating to the subject of our inquiry, we cannot find any conflict between him and the witnesses examined before us as to any matter of fact relevant to our inquiry. ...

Statement of 12th July 1907

## Sir Arthur Vicars

I am in charge of the Office of Arms, Dublin Castle. The jewels were last cleaned about the end of January 1907 in the strongroom, the grill being locked during the time they were cleaning them. They were cleaned by two men from Wests, College-green, and were carefully examined by me, and I took possession of them from the men.

The jewels were last worn by His Excellency on 15th March 1907, after which I brought them back and placed them in the safe in the Library.

About the end of March last, Mr Burtchaell asked me if I had any objection to show the jewels to Mrs Tarleton and her daughter, of Kilkenny, who are cousins of his. I showed the diamonds to Mrs Tarleton and her daughter and a lady friend of theirs. I might have shown the diamonds to another lady friend between March and 11th June.

On 11th June I showed the diamonds to Mr J.C. Hodgson, FSA, Librarian to the Duke of Northumberland at Alnwick Castle, along with one collar. From 11th June to 6th July I have no recollection of seeing the jewels, nor of having gone to the safe. The gold collars were last worn at the investiture of the Earl of Meath on 14th April 1905.

The case which contained Lord Ormonde's and Lord Howth's collars were not inspected since April 1905, but Lord Mayor's and Lord Enniskillen's were certainly inspected by me within this year.

On 17th June I wrote to Lady de Ros asking to forward the collar of her late husband to me, stating that if she had it at her address that she could forward it by Parcel Post, registered, or if in London that it might be sent to West & Son, College-green. The collar was sent from Garrard & Co. to West on 24th June, and West acknowledged the receipt of collar, and I then wrote instructing them to have Lord de Ros's name and date of investiture engraved on it. I did not hear any more about the collar until I found it on my table in the office about 11 a.m. on 6th July 1907.

About 3.30 p.m. on 6th July I gave the collar and a bunch of keys to Stivey, the messenger, to carry down the collar to the safe. I pointed out the key of the safe to Stivey, and this is the only occasion I ever gave it to him. I followed him down about a minute afterwards, and found him at the safe with the door still closed. Stivey informed me that the safe was unlocked, because he could not get the key into the proper slot. I said 'Impossible' - knowing well the great precautions I always took when locking the safe. I then opened the safe, which was unlocked, the handle being turned down, which would represent to outside observation that the safe was locked.

I removed the case which always contained the Crown diamonds, and my worst fears were aroused by the lightness of the case and the fact that the key was in the lock, which was never so left by me. On opening the case I found the diamond star and badge had been removed, but the badge ribbon and clasp were placed in the centre, having been removed from the badge. This could not be done hurriedly, as it involved unscrewing a swivel and coaxing the ribbon off the hook.

On further examination I found the collars of Lord Mayo, Lord Enniskillen, Lord Ormonde and Lord Howth missing from the cases, and the late Lord Cork's collar and enamelled badge gone from its deal box, which only contained the tissue paper in which it had been wrapped. The small box containing my mother's jewels as described was also gone, and the only thing left was my patent under which I hold office. The box which contained my mother's jewels was locked, and my brother, Mr G. Mahony, had the key.

I remained at the safe and sent my messenger to the Commissioners of Police to ask one of them to come at once; also to inform the Detective Department.

So far as I know there are only two keys for the safe, which are always in my custody, except in 1902, when I sent one from London in the Chief Secretary's pouch to the Under-Secretary to give to Mr Blake to bring the jewels to London, where they were required by His Excellency. Mr Blake returned me the key in London, having had it only one day in his possession.

The key of the safe which I use I always carry with me along with other keys on a steel ring, except on full dress nights, when I remove it from the bunch and carry it on a ring of its own in my uniform coat pocket; the other key for safe I have always kept concealed in my residence. I have never left the safe keys in my office or other place where any person could get possession of them.

There are four keys for the strongroom - one kept by myself, one by the messenger, one by Mr Mahony and one by Mr Burtchaell, which latter, for the past year, has been kept concealed in the strongroom.

My key of the strongroom I always carry on my watch chain, which is placed under my pillow at night. I recollect leaving the key of the safe in my writing table at my residence about two months ago, but the keys, with safe key included, were brought to me to my office by my servant, Frederick Pitt, within an hour. The keys were found by my maidservant in my writing desk, and she directed Pitt to bring them to the Castle to me.

Elizabeth Darcy is the servant. Frederick Pitt, 17 years, is the male servant. His father is coachman with Rev. Alfred Wellington Ingram of Enville Rectory, Stourbridge.

Mr M'Ennery, junior, of Rooskey House, Dunboyne, stayed in my house for one night on the 2nd July.

A man named Riley Walker, 19 years of age, stayed at my house for a fortnight in April last and is at present servant with Sir Kildare Burrows, Kildare. He came to my house to learn his duties as footman under my footman, Frederick Pitt. Walker never visited the Office of Arms, nor had he any knowledge of the keys of the safe.

Arthur Phillips, my coachman, has a wife and four children, and resides in Clonskeagh Terrace He is seven years in my employment. He had access to my keys about eleven months ago, and occasionally visited the Library in the Office of Arms. He frequently saw the jewel case with me, and often saw me go into the Office of Arms with the cases.

The office staff are Mr Shackleton, Dublin Herald; Mr Mahony, Cork Herald; Mr Bennett Goldney, Athlone (the Mayor of Canterbury); Mr Burtchaell, Mr Horlock, Miss Gibbon, Mr Stivey, and Mrs Farrell and her son James, coal carrier.

Mr Burtchaell is in my employment since I took up office. Mr Horlock is in my employment since January last. I engaged him in London, and got a high character of him from his clergy. It was through an advertisement in one of the papers (a London paper) I got acquainted with him. When he came to Dublin he stayed for a short time in my house until he got lodgings. He gave me his address as 13 Railway Approach, Lower Edmonton, London.

On Wednesday 3rd July, to the best of my recollection, I arrived at the office at 12 noon and left about 6 p.m. Stivey informed me that he was told by Mrs Farrell, the office cleaner, that she found the hall door open when she arrived to clean the office in the morning.

On Friday 5th July I left the office at 7.15 p.m. About 5.45 p.m. Stivey asked me whether he could go, and I said 'Yes'. He asked me whether he should lock the strongroom, and I told him to do so, at the same time handing him a manuscript to be replaced therein. I subsequently had occasion to pass the strongroom door to go to the telephone, more than once, and the door was closed.

At 7.10 p.m. I was leaving the office with Horlock, and in the hall said to him in a joking way: 'Wait a minute till I make my usual tour of inspection.' I then passed through the Library, glancing at all the bookcases, and satisfied myself they were closed. I passed into the messenger's room and noticed the window was bolted, tried the handle of the strongroom door and found the door was locked. I then passed into the hall and joined Horlock. As we were going out of the door I met a press reporter, who gave me some information which necessitated my telephoning to the Vice-Regal Lodge. I parted from Horlock and the pressman (having previously closed the office door and assured myself that it was locked) and went to the telephone in the Chief Secretary's office and subsequently went home. On Saturday 6th July I arrived at the office at about 11 a.m. I have a vague recollection of being told by Stivey that Mrs Farrell had found the strongroom door open when she arrived, but at the time I did not realize that it was that morning, and being very busy left the matter for subsequent investigation.

It was not until Sunday afternoon, when I was working at my house in connection with the royal visit with Horlock, that I realized that the strongroom door was open on Saturday morning. I said to Horlock that I must ask Stivey this point in the morning.

Horlock had informed me at my house on Sunday that Stivey had told me in my office on Saturday that the strongroom door was found open that morning.

There was nothing missing from the strongroom, although three gold collars and badges were exposed in a plate glass press, locked with four locks, besides two state maces, the sword of state, a jewelled sceptre, a crown and two massive silver spurs. There was a gold collar elsewhere in the strongroom.

I do not suggest any single one of my staff had anything to do with it, nor do I suspect my maidservant or footman, nor any person who slept in my house.

My theory is that some person got wax impressions of the keys, a few seconds would suffice to do this. Having regard to the great precautions taken by me in the custody of these keys, I cannot entertain the idea that the actual key of the safe was utilized by the thieves.

(Signed)
Arthur Vicars, Ulster
12th July 1907

I went to London about 23rd December 1906 and returned to Dublin on 7th January 1907, during which time Mr Burchaell and Mr Mahony were in charge, but I had my safe key with me.

I was away from 25th January, at Naas, and Mr Mahony was in charge in office. On 20th and 21st March I was absent at Palmerstown, and Mr Mahony was in charge.

The office was closed from Good Friday, 29th March, to 2nd April, also on 4th May and from Whit Monday to Whit Tuesday, when I was at Ballyfin, the residence of Sir Algernon Coote.

(Signed)
Arthur Vicars, Ulster

## Supplementary Statement of 18th July 1907

Referring to my statement of 12th July 1907, for the last few years it was my custom on occasions of full dress nights, when the jewels were worn, to detach my safe key from my private bunch at my residence and put it in the tail pocket of my tunic. The bunch I then left in my uniform overcoat pocket, and also the office door key loose.

Since Mr Naramore left the Castle I have always hung my uniform overcoat behind the door of His Excellency's Private Secretary's room. Prior to that I always left my uniform overcoat hanging in Mr Naramore's room. I thought I had made this clear when reporting the matter to the police on 6th July.

The key of the strongroom door, on these nights, I always left on my watch chain, with any money, etc., in my dressing-table drawer, duly locked, the key of which was on my bunch.

When making my usual tour of inspection every evening I do not try if the presses are locked. I merely walk through the rooms to see that the presses with spring locks are closed to, but I never try the safe door handle, as I always test it when locking it, and I seldom have occasion to open it. I always, however, look at the window-bolts, especially in Mr Burtchaell's room, and Mr Stivey and I never fail to try the strongroom handle.

I can assign no reason for giving Stivey the safe key on the 6th July, beyond the fact that I was for the moment engaged with a letter, and the collar and case I wished him to carry down. At any rate, I followed Stivey down, and when I entered the Library Stivey had not even opened the safe. My recollection is that he was in a stooped position at it, having just ascertained that the safe was unlocked.

The keys in the key box only had reference to bookcases and drawers with papers. It also contained the duplicate key of the grill itself when the strongroom was locked, as the grill was only locked in the daytime. I have a key for the key box; Mr Horlock has another; and I believe that Mr Burtchaell has the third.

The spare key of the strongroom is kept concealed in one of the drawers at the very back, wrapped in paper. This is the key that Mr Burtchaell gave up some time ago. I and Stivey used to lock up the place and leave together up to Xmas 1906. Since that time I have generally let him off at 5.30 p.m., on account of having Mr Horlock in the office with me to do anything that was required. Stivey and I were the only persons, so far as I knew, who knew that the spare key of the strongroom was concealed in the drawer there.

(Signed)
Arthur vicars, Ulster
18th July 1907

Day One: Friday 10th January 1908

*His Honour Judge James Johnston Shaw, KC, Robert Fitzwilliam Starkie, Esquire, and Chester Jones, Esquire, Commissioners, appointed by His Excellency the Lord Lieutenant to investigate the circumstances of the loss of the Regalia of the Order of St Patrick, and to inquire whether Sir Arthur Vicars exercised due vigilance and proper care as the custodian thereof held their first sitting in the Office of Arms, Dublin Castle, on Friday, the 10th day of January 1908 with Mr C.T. Beard, ISO as Secretary.*

*Sir Arthur Vicars, Ulster King of Arms, was present, with his solicitor, Mr Meredith, and his counsel, the Right Hon. J.H. Campbell, KC, and Mr Timothy Healy, KC. The Solicitor-General, instructed by Mr Malachi Kelly, Chief Crown Solicitor, was also present. The Vice-Regal Warrant was read by Mr Beard.*

Campbell: Might I state, sir, that I appear here, together with my friend, Mr Healy, and so far as may be necessary, on behalf of Sir Arthur Vicars, but I would wish to be informed, sir, by you at the outset whether it is intended to conduct these proceedings in public or in private?

Chairman: Well, the intention, I think, was to conduct the proceedings in private, but we are ready to hear any application that may be made as to that.

Campbell: Am I right, also, sir, in the belief that we entertain that under the warrant appointing you, you have no power to compel the attendance of witnesses and no power to examine witnesses on oath?

Chairman: Well, I understand that that is so.

Campbell: Well, it is only right and fair, sir, that at the outset I should exactly define the position that we intend to take up under these circumstances on behalf of Sir Arthur Vicars, who would not, nor would his counsel, ever willingly be a party to a private or secret inquiry, to start with. The matter has now been the subject of public comment for six months. During that six months it is notorious - for we do not come here without knowing what is going on around us - it is notorious that reports and rumours of a most extraordinary character and nature have been most freely circulated; and, apart from these reports, it is also within the knowledge of Sir Arthur Vicars and his advisers that in connection with the disappearance of these Crown Jewels other charges have been suggested and insinuated by the authorities against Sir Arthur Vicars of a very shocking and a very grave character. And it is also known to Sir Arthur Vicars - in fact, it was so stated to his brother, Mr Mahony, by the Chief Secretary - that these other matters to which I have referred have been laid before His Majesty, and were before him.

Now, there is no doubt, as I have said, that in connection with the disappearance of these jewels very terrible suggestions and insinuations have been made affecting the moral character of Sir Arthur Vicars. They have never been formulated. He has repeatedly asked for them. He has declared his readiness and his anxiety to meet them. He has asked to see them, and he has asked to know what they are. He has been met with evasion throughout.

It is his own opinion and that of his friends, and his counsel and attorney agree with him in regard to that, that no inquiry in connection with the disappearance of these jewels can ever be satisfactory either in the interests of justice or of ordinary fair play, particularly to an official with his record, a record of some 15 years of public service, the merits of which have been acknowledged over and over again by successive Lord Lieutenants, that it would be an intolerable act of injustice to have an inquiry which, on the face of it, would appear to exclude these matters, though, as I have said, it is notorious that they were part and parcel of the information upon which action was taken in the month of October last, by writing to Sir Arthur Vicars - because I do not know whether you, gentlemen, are aware of it, that on the 23rd of October last he got an intimation from the Lord Lieutenant to say that His Majesty had come to the conclusion that he would reconstitute this office, and that his services were no longer in regard.

Chairman: Your argument is not an objection to the privacy of the inquiry, but an objection to the inquiry altogether.

Campbell: If you look, sir, at your warrant, it is very peculiar in the form of it, because if it was proposed to limit it it would have been quite sufficient to have said that you were to inquire whether Sir Arthur Vicars exercised due vigilance in regard to the custody of the jewels, but that is not what it says. It puts in the forefront not that, but to investigate the circumstances of the loss of the regalia; and I may tell you that one of the charges formulated against Sir Arthur Vicars, nor formulated, but insinuated against him, in connection with the disappearance of the jewels, is an allegation that he introduced an undesirable person into the privacy of his office.

I only wish to make it perfectly plain that Sir Arthur Vicars neither now nor at any time has tried to avoid a public judicial inquiry. He has courted it, and has been most anxious for it, and he has been defamed by aspersions of the most infamous character which have never been formulated, which, though they have been made behind his back, he has had no opportunities of having publicly investigated and they have been denied to him.

*The rest of the first day's discussions - and the results of the ensuing considerations of the Committee - were summarized by the Chairman when the proceedings reconvened at 11.00 a.m. on Saturday 11th January.*

Day Two: Saturday 11th January 1908

Chairman: At the sitting of this Commission yesterday morning, Mr J.H. Campbell, KC, as counsel for Sir Arthur Vicars, asked whether this inquiry was to be public or private. We stated that we were prepared to hear any application he might make for a public inquiry, and consider and determine it. He then proceeded, as we understood, to urge reasons why the inquiry should be public. As most of his arguments seemed to us to be based upon the terms of reference in our Warrant, and upon the absence of any power in a vice-regal commission to compel the attendance of witnesses or to administer an oath, we pointed out that these objections to the scope of the inquiry and the powers of the Commission would apply to a public, as much as to a private inquiry. Mr Campbell then said that under no circumstances could Sir Arthur Vicars take any part in an inquiry whose scope was restricted to the question of his own want of due diligence and care in the custody of the insignia of St Patrick, and which was not a public judicial investigation with power in the Court to compel the attendance of witnesses and examine them upon oath. He was then asked if he withdrew his application for a public inquiry. He said that he did, and that he wished to announce the withdrawal of Sir Arthur Vicars from any further part in the present inquiry. He was asked if that meant that Sir Arthur Vicars would refuse to attend as a witness, and to give the Commission any information he might have on the subject of the inquiry. Mr Campbell replied that if Sir Arthur Vicars took the advice of his counsel he would not attend or assist the Commission in any way.

Under these circumstances we thought it our duty to adjourn the Commission in order that we might consider what course we ought to take in the situation that had thus arisen. After careful consideration we were disposed to think that in the absence of Sir Arthur Vicars, who is the only person directly interested in the result of our inquiry, and without the information which he could give us as the responsible custodian of the jewels which have been lost, any further prosecution of this inquiry could effect no useful purpose, and that we should so report to His Excellency.

We do not wish, however, to come to any final decision on this matter until we have heard from the Solicitor-General the view which the government which he represents take as to the further proceedings of this Commission. If he is able to show us that this inquiry, under the circumstances which have arisen, is likely to lead to any useful result, we are quite prepared to proceed, and to do our best with the evidence at our disposal.

Solicitor-general: Well, sir, we have carefully considered the situation that has arisen out of the statement that was made by my learned friend Mr Campbell yesterday, and, as I understand, the position now is this, that Sir Arthur Vicars, who was custodian of the jewels at the time of their loss, has definitely declined to come forward and give any evidence on the subject of your inquiry or to facilitate the Commission in any way. The importance of that decision and the responsibility involved in it are obvious. I recognize that you have no power to compel him to give evidence, but the government consider that the inquiry should certainly nevertheless go forward, and that the relevant evidence otherwise available should be received.

Now as to that evidence, this Commission is not appointed and could not be appointed as a court of criminal investigation. Its function, however, is, as I understand it, to investigate and report on all the facts bearing on the loss of the jewels, and on the question of Sir Arthur Vicars' care and vigilance as their custodian, and on whether or not those facts may throw or tend to throw light on the question of the person who abstracted them.

The inquiry is not as I understand by any means limited to the mere question of whether or not Sir Arthur Vicars was negligent in his office as custodian, and I, sir, am in a position with the information supplied to me to present a number of witnesses to the Commission who will be able to give important and relevant evidence upon both those subject matters of inquiry, and with your permission, sir, I propose to present those witnesses for examination according to such procedure as the Commission may lay down. Possibly the more convenient course would be - inasmuch as I am apprised of the general bearing of the evidence which the witnesses are able to give the Commission may think it proper that I should in the first instance, at any rate, by a series of questions to them indicate the nature of that information, leaving it to the Commission afterwards to put such supplementary questions as they may think proper. But, of course, that is a matter entirely for the decision of the Commission.

Chairman: We are still of opinion that the main object of inquiry under this Commission is the absence or the presence of due vigilance and care on the part of Sir Arthur Vicars in the custody of these jewels. Of course, we see and saw from the beginning that in order to arrive at that it was necessary for us to have before us the whole of the circumstances under which the jewels were abstracted, because it is impossible to say what part of the evidence bearing upon those circumstances may not also bear upon the want of due care and vigilance on the part of Sir Arthur Vicars, and we think that any evidence that is relevant to the first part of the inquiry, that is to say the circumstances under which the jewels were lost, must also be relevant to the second part of the inquiry, which is the main gist of the inquiry.

We think also that as we are not in possession of any of the evidence, and have no idea of what evidence any witness is likely to give upon the subject, the proper course would be for the Solicitor-General to put proper questions, not in any way in the sense of cross-examination, but to bring out whatever evidence the witnesses have to give us. We, of course, the members of the Commission here, may then seek, for ourselves, for any further information.

Solicitor-general: Well, sir, the first matter I wish to direct the attention of the Commission to is the Statutes of the Order of St Patrick that were established by order dated the 29th July 1905 in the fifth year of the present King, Statutes that are appointed by virtue of Letters Patent passed by His Majesty dealing with the Order and with the very custody of these jewels. The 27th Statute provides that 'it is ordained that Our Ulster King of Arms for the time being shall be the King of Arms, Knight Attendant on the Order, and shall have the custody of the Seal and of the Archives of the Order and the jewelled Insignia of the Grand Master'.

Now, the jewelled insignia of the Grand Master, which, of course, means the jewels that were abstracted here - for these were the important jewels that were abstracted or a portion of them - are by Statute 12 defined. That Statute says: 'It is ordained that in pursuance of the Royal Ordinance of Our Royal Predecessor King William the Fourth, bearing date the 7th March 1831, the jewelled Insignia of the Grand Master made by Command of His said late Majesty for the use of the Grand Master of the Most Illustrious Order, of which a description is hereunto annexed and which are Crown Jewels shall be handed over by each Lord Lieutenant-General and General Governor of Ireland, Grand Master of the said Most Illustrious Order, to his successor at such time, as the Sword of State is delivered over, and shall be deposited by Our Ulster King of Arms in the Chancery of the Order along with the other Insignia of the Order.' The other insignia of the Order were the badges and collars worn by the knight companions, and some of these collars, it is common knowledge, were part of the jewels abstracted on the occasion.

Now, by Statute 37 the Chancery is defined with a declaration that: 'We are further pleased to ordain that the Chancery of the said Most Illustrious Order wherein a record of all proceedings connected therewith shall be carefully deposited and preserved shall be the Office of Arms in Our Castle of Dublin.'

Chairman: That is the office we are now sitting in?

Solicitor-general: Yes, the office we are now sitting in. And the method of deposit and custody is provided by Statute 20.

Chairman: You do not make any application, Solicitor, for a public inquiry in this case?

Solicitor-general: No. I was at the Commission yesterday, and I made no application at all for a public inquiry. I was saying that the method of deposit is provided by clause 20 of the Statutes, which says: 'It is further ordained that the said Collars and Badges shall be deposited for safe keeping in a steel safe in the strongroom in the Chancery of the Order in the Office of Arms in Ireland until they are disposed of by the Grand Master.' In that way, as I understand, the Ulster King of Arms becomes their custodian, and is obliged under the Statute to deposit them in a steel safe in the strongroom of the Chancery of the Order, which is the present office in which we are sitting. Now, sir, with regard to the collars - and this is a matter that will arise, I think, in the course of the inquiry - it is provided that in the case of the death of one of the knight companions of the Order certain steps shall be taken. By clause 19 it is provided that 'on the decease of each and every Knight Companion of this Order, the heirs, executors and administrators of such Knight Companions shall, within three months after the decease of any such Knight, deliver the before-mentioned Collars and Badges to the Sovereign or the Grand Master for the service of the Order. And Ulster King of Arms, or his Deputy, shall have full power in the name of the Grand Master to apply to the heirs, executors and administrators of such deceased Knights for the Collars and Badges aforesaid.' That is clause 19, and then, as I have read to you, by clause 20, having got them, apparently it is his duty to deposit them with the other insignia in a safe in the strongroom of the Chancery of the Order.

That, as I understand the Statutes, is the position defining the obligation under which Ulster is to have charge of the jewels. As I understand, sir, as far as I am able to make out with the assistance of my friends there were no previous statutes which expressly dealt with the custody of the insignia of the Grand Master. But that Statute, passed in 1905, is perfectly decisive on the matter.

Jones: I did not quite follow the section you read. It says the collars and badges shall be deposited in a steel safe. Does that include the insignia of the Grand Master?

Solicitor-general: It does, because by a previous clause it is provided that the jewelled insignia are to be kept with the other insignia, and the other insignia it is provided are to be kept in that way.

*The Solicitor-General then proceeded to examine Mr George Burtchaell, Secretary to Sir Arthur Vicars in the Office of Arms since 1893; Mrs Mary Farrell, the office cleaner for the last four years, who confirmed that she had seen a 'strange gentleman' in the office in the spring of 1907, some four to six months prior to the discovery of the robbery; and Mr William Stivey, the messenger in the office from April 1901 to October 1907.*

Day Three: Monday 13th July 1908

## Examination of Mr Peirce Gun Mahony

*Mr Peirce Mahony, son of Mr Peirce O'Mahony and nephew of Sir Arthur Vicars, was appointed Cork Herald of Arms of the Order of St Patrick in September 1905. He lived in Dublin and, as a volunteer, attended the Office of Arms 'as often as he could'. He affirmed that he was given a latchkey for the outer door of the office and a strongroom key when his uncle was away but had not returned them when Sir Arthur came back from vacation in December 1906.*

Solicitor-general: Did you on those previous occasions before Christmas 1906, when you might have had the latchkey, receive a strongroom key under the same conditions as you got the latchkey, that is to say, during the temporary absence of Sir Arthur Vicars?

Mahony: Yes. If I had it at all.

Solicitor-general: And does the same evidence apply to the strongroom key – that upon Sir Arthur Vicars' return you would restore the strongroom key to him with the latch key; was that your practice up to Christmas 1906?

Mahony: Yes. Yes, if I had it at all.

Solicitor-general: Now, you have told us that on Sir Arthur Vicars' return after that Christmas vacation of 1906 you did not give up the latchkey. And you have told us that you kept it apparently to provide yourself with easy access to the office when you were coming here. What was the need of your having the strongroom key?

Mahony: Well, when I came in here, you see, in the morning I could unlock the strongroom door if anybody else was in and let them get out the books.

Solicitor-general: For what purpose could the strongroom door require to be opened before 11 in the morning?

Mahony: None that I know of.

Solicitor-general: Did he (Sir Arthur Vicars) ever discuss with you at all the propriety of your being allowed to keep it?

Mahony: Well, I think he considered as an official that I ought to have a key. That is the only thing.

Solicitor-general: While you were here on the 4th of July, Thursday, and also on Friday 5th July was Mr Shackleton in the office at all?

Mahony: Not that I know of.

Solicitor-general: Do you know Mr Goldney?

Mahony: I know him now. I did not meet Mr Goldney till either the Monday or Tuesday after the discovery of the robbery.

Solicitor-general: Then I may take it from you that Mr Goldney was not in the office on Thursday or Friday, the 4th or 5th of July, respectively?

Mahony: No; I did not see him.

Solicitor-general: Now, the robbery was discovered, we know, on the Saturday 6th July. When after the discovery did you see your key of the strongroom?

Mahony: Oh, when I went back that Saturday evening. We were late, of course, that evening – I took those two keys from where I had left them, and I took them round that evening, and handed them over to Sir Arthur Vicars.

Solicitor-general: I take it then that your strongroom key was in your drawer at home. Was it locked up in the desk?

Mahony: Oh, yes, as far as I remember it was locked.

Chairman: And if any witness said that on the morning on which this occurrence took place your key of the strongroom door was locked up in the strongroom wrapped up in oiled paper, can you give any explanation of that?

Mahony: That someone had stated this? Well, I should have said that they had made a mistake, because there was another key. I understand that there were four keys. So I should say simply that they were confusing.

Chairman: You arrived in Dublin on the morning of Wednesday 3rd July. You came to the office the next day, the 4th July?

Mahony: Yes.

Chairman: And did anybody in the office tell you that the outer door had been unlocked on the morning of Wednesday 3rd?

Mahony: No. Nobody told me that. I am quite certain of that.

Chairman: Was anything said to you about the strongroom door having been found open on the morning of the Saturday?

Mahony: Not a word.

Chairman: What time did you come in on Saturday?

Mahony: I remember I had considerable difficulty when I was giving information last July in remembering exactly when I came in that morning, but it was between eleven and twelve.

Chairman: How long did you remain in the office that day?

Mahony: On that Saturday? Oh, very late.

Chairman: Before you gave up the key to Sir Arthur Vicars in the evening, had there been any conversation between you and

Sir Arthur Vicars about the strongroom (having been found open)?

Mahony: Oh, no. Not that I can remember.

Chairman: Was the circumstance ever mentioned to you at all?

Mahony: Oh, no. Not on the Saturday. I know that the messenger, when I came in, never said a word about it, because he generally keeps my letters and things there on a little table, and when I walk in in the morning it is my custom to go and get them and then go upstairs. That is, I mean, whatever might come to me personally as distinguished from the office.

Chairman: Well, after the discovery of course Sir Arthur Vicars told you about the jewels being lost on the Saturday?

Mahony: Well, I do not know how exactly to answer. But may I explain what happened about the matter? I was upstairs. Sir Arthur Vicars called me once or twice, and I think I had just come back from lunch or something, and I came downstairs and came in here, and I found him looking ghastly white, with the case, I think it is morocco, in which these jewels were kept, open, and he said 'Gone'! or something like that.

Chairman: Then, of course, you had some conversation about how possibly they could have been abstracted?

Mahony: I am afraid I do not remember what took place, or what we said.

Chairman: He did not ask you where your keys were, or whether anybody could have had access to your key?

Mahony: Oh, I am certain he did not, and I am prepared to swear that, and another thing, I do not suppose it occurred to him to ask, because it was not the strongroom that we discovered the loss in. It was here, the safe, and I had no key of that safe.

Solicitor-general: Is there any book in the office, Mr Mahony, recording the attendance of the officials – the Heralds, Pursuivant or other officials of the office?

Mahony: Not that I know.

Starkie: Is there an official diary kept by any officials in the office?

Mahony: In the strongroom there is some book for entries.

Starkie: But, is there no personal official diary kept by the officials?

Mahony: No, I do not keep a diary myself; and I am sorry, sir, that I did not, now. But these official entries are more in relation to the official work, so that things may be put on record for others afterwards. There is a letter book, of course, that will tell a good deal which would help you as regards the date. Should I remember any other things I will tell you.

*The next person to be examined by the Solicitor-General was Mr John O'Keeffe, an employee of the Board of Works, who visited the Office of Arms for the purpose of lighting the clock in the tower, the last occasion having been on 24th March 1907. He confirmed that he had a key for the outer door and then simply walked upstairs to the tower; he had no occasion to enter any of the other rooms in the Office of Arms. After the jewels were stolen he handed his key over to Detective Officer Kerr of G Division.*

### Examination of Detective Officer Owen Kerr

*Detective Officer Kerr confirmed that he had been doing duty in connection with Dublin Castle for the past five years. His tasks were to inspect the various offices – the State Apartments; the terrace of buildings known as La Touche's Bank; this office; the Chief Secretary's office and all connected with it, and private residences of court officials when they are open, when anyone is employed in them – to inspect them, and see that all is correct, that there are no fires in the place, that there is nothing dangerous to the building and that no one is concealed. He had held keys for the various offices it was his duty to inspect for the past five years.*

Solicitor-general: Now, you remember Friday night, the 5th of July? What time did you come that evening to make your inspection?

Kerr: Well, soon after seven o'clock.

Solicitor-general: And did you observe anyone present in any single office?

Kerr: No, sir; the blinds drawn and place still.

Solicitor-general: When you say shortly after seven, can you give the Commission any idea of about how soon after seven it was?

Kerr: Well, when I had my inspection of this house finished I went out to the barrack, where I reside, and remained there more than an hour, because I paused and thought the Chief Secretary's office would not be vacant at the time, at least all the officials would not have been gone, and the office cleaners. There come in office cleaners to those offices, it being their duty to attend, and I always went round when the office cleaners had cleared out. I would fix it that the inspection was finished at half past seven. Well, I might be five minutes astray. I do not often look at my watch, but generally my time at that hour of the evening is very well gauged.

Solicitor-general: Well, when you were making your inspection that Friday evening, did you come into this room?

Kerr: I did, sir; in fact it was the first room that I came into.

Solicitor-general: Did you know at that time whether the safe contained jewels?

Kerr: I had no knowledge that jewels were there; I knew that the gold collars were there.

Solicitor-general: Did you make any examination at all on that evening to see whether the safe was locked or not?

Kerr: Well, I saw the handle in its normal position dropped or down, so that it was not disturbed, and it was always locked. I sometimes tested it, but I did not test it on that evening. It was only when workmen or strangers would be employed in this office that I tested the presses and doors, and looked for papers that might be strewn about, or portable property that might be carried off.

Solicitor-general: Did you see that strongroom door that Friday night?

Kerr: I did, sir.

Solicitor-general: When you saw it was it open or locked?

Kerr: It was closed and bolted, and I am sure it was locked. I have always got the habit of jerking it to the right to see and I could not swear I jerked it to the right on that occasion, but I feel sure that I did.

Solicitor-general: But as to the position it was, was it closed too?

Kerr: It was, and bolted, with the handle down; and I am almost positively sure that I jerked the handle to the right to see that it was locked.

Solicitor-general: Do you remember Saturday 6th July, the date of the discovery?

Kerr: I do, sir.

Solicitor-general: When on that, date did you hear that something was wrong in the office?

Kerr: Well, about ten minutes or fifteen past four.

Solicitor-general: Who was here?

Kerr: Sir Arthur Vicars was here, the Assistant Commissioner of the Dublin Metropolitan Police, Superintendent Lowe, Mr Mahony and, I think, Mr Horlock and Mr Burtchaell. Stivey came to the door when he heard me at it; but I do not know whether he followed me in.

Solicitor-general: Had the opening of the outer door – the fact that the outer door was found open on the Wednesday morning – been reported to you at all?

Kerr: No, sir.

Solicitor-general: When first did you hear that from anyone?

Kerr: I heard it about three o'clock on Sunday 7th July, from Mrs Farrell, the office cleaner, at her own house.

Solicitor-general: Coming to that occasion on the Saturday, when you came into this room do you remember that when you came into the room Sir Arthur Vicars addressed you?

Kerr: He did, sir. He said: 'Kerr, the jewels are all gone; some of the smart boys that have been over for the King's visit made a clean sweep of them.'

Solicitor-general: Did he tell you how the safe came to be discovered unlocked?

Kerr: He did. I then asked him one question – I did not think it proper to ask many questions when my superior officers were present – but I ventured to ask one question: 'How did it come to be open?' And Sir Arthur Vicars said: 'The Board of Works again; I have asked them for a good safe, for which I have correspondence to show, and they refused it and they did not give it to me; I have no confidence in this safe.' Then after describing how it was found out he said: 'I sent Stivey with a collar' – he used two letters of the alphabet, I don't know exactly what they were, 'SS' or something like that, I forget the two noblemen's names, Lord Enniskillen or Lord Erne, but since I understand it is Lord de Ros – 'and he came and found it open'. And then Stivey, whether he was in the room or coming in after me or not, came forward and described how he found it open.

Starkie: When did you first hear that the strongroom door had been found open?

Kerr: At about three o'clock on Sunday 7th July, from Mrs Farrell, the office cleaner.

Jones: At the same time that she told you about the outer door being open on the Wednesday?

Kerr: Yes, sir. I learned the two at the same time, and learned from her also that she had reported to Sir Arthur Vicars, reported both incidents to Sir Arthur Vicars through Stivey, the messenger.

Solicitor-general: Now, do you remember anything being said on that occasion here about the diamonds, and what would result if they were offered for sale?

Kerr: There was some remark made by somebody – I do not know who 'Could the diamonds be identified?' ... And Sir Arthur Vicars said: 'If they are offered for sale, it will lead to their recovery, as West's people, I inquired from them some time ago in case they were lost or stolen could they be identified, and I was informed they could, even out of their setting. Brazilian diamonds.'

Solicitor-general: Did Sir Arthur Vicars say anything on that occasion about a conversation he had with Sir George Holmes, chairman of the Board of Works?

Kerr: He did, sir. And these were the words so far as I recollect: 'I met Sir George Holmes at a party', and I think he mentioned the word party, 'and I told him in conversation that I would not be responsible for the custody of the state jewels unless he supplied a proper safe.'

Solicitor-general: Now, did you inspect the Office of Arms on that Saturday evening. And again on Sunday 7th July?

Kerr: I did, sir. I examined the sashes and the outer doors and windows.

Solicitor-general: Did you find in the vicinity of the safe here any parcel or paper apparently that had been used for the purpose of wrapping jewels belonging to Sir Arthur Vicars' family, that were said to have been abstracted?

Kerr: There was a heap of old papers below in the basement, and Sir Arthur Vicars described and said his brother's jewellery was stolen out of a parcel, he said a sealed parcel, and would know it at once. He had no entry of them, he said; it was a sealed parcel, wrapped in brown paper, and I looked to see if I could get the parcel of brown paper in which it was wrapped.

Solicitor-general: Did you find any trace of it?

Kerr: No, I did not find any trace of it.

Solicitor-general: On Monday 8th of July, you came here by direction of Superintendent Lowe? And there was an expert on that day to examine the lock of the strongroom?

Kerr: Oh, yes. I was directed to do that, and I went and brought Mr O'Hare, the manager of Milner's Safe Agency in Dublin.

Solicitor-general: Did you see him try the strongroom door?

Kerr: He did, sir.

Solicitor-general: Was the safe here from which the jewels were taken guarded from the morning of the 8th July till the morning of the 9th July?

Kerr: In consequence of something Milner's man said, there was a constable on duty here, and he was to allow no one to tamper with it in any way. There was a constable on duty all the time. A guard was mounted over the safe by Superintendent Lowe.

Solicitor-general: And it was also examined by the expert?

Kerr: That was on the following morning, Tuesday morning.

Solicitor-general: Did you on the morning of Tuesday make a minute search?

Kerr: Yes, accompanied by Sir Arthur Vicars; all the offices, and the presses and every piece of furniture in the place.

Solicitor-general: In making that minute search, was there any trace at all of a forcible entry?

Kerr: No trace of a forcible entry.

Solicitor-general: And were the jewels searched for in every hole and corner of the place?

Kerr: Every hole and corner of the place, and we examined the doors and windows very carefully.

Solicitor-general: Were the coal cellars examined?

Kerr: They were examined superficially at first, and then the

Board of Works got a man to turn the coal over grain after grain, and it was all thrown out of the cellars and put back again; that was only in cellars where there was any coal. I turned it over with the shovel myself.

Solicitor-general: You heard nothing, as I understand, till Saturday evening about the strongroom at all being open. … And the next day, Monday 8th, you had a conversation with Sir Arthur Vicars on the subject, had you?

Kerr: I had, and Stivey was present.

Solicitor-general: Tell the Commission, if you please, in your own way, what that conversation was?

Kerr: Sir Arthur Vicars was aware that the police had learned that the door was found open on the Saturday morning, but I do not know how he conveyed to me that he did hear it. I am under the impression that he was visited by the officers investigating the case. I said: 'It is a wonder that you didn't report the finding of the door of the strongroom open on Saturday morning even after the jewels had been missed.' 'Oh', he said, 'I was so thronged owing to the preparing for the King's visit.'

I then asked him how many keys there were in existence for the strongroom door. And he named every person who possessed a key on Friday and Saturday. He said there were four keys. 'I have one; Mr Mahony has one; Stivey has one; and one is locked up in the strongroom itself.' He continued the conversation and said that when Mr Mahony was going on holidays he gave him his key 'and I deposited it in the strongroom and he has not yet taken it over'.

That struck me and I asked him: 'How is it that Mr Mahony – after he has returned to work to the office for some days – has not resumed possession of his key.' And Stivey spoke up and said: 'Though Mr Mahony has returned to the office he only puts in an appearance and seldom has occasion to enter the strongroom.' That satisfied my mind.

I then put the other question: 'Were the keys in the strongroom now there or were they found there this morning and did you examine them?' And Sir Arthur said: 'Yes; everything in the strongroom is correct.' I said, addressing Mr Stivey: 'Has your key or any of those other two keys being missing any time lately?' And he said: 'No.' That satisfied me that the four keys were satisfactorily accounted for on those dates and I did not ask to see them, because Sir Arthur Vicars said they were found correct and that satisfied my mind and disposed of the four keys.

*The Solicitor-General said the next witness he proposed to examine was Mr Horlock, and he asked Mr Beard (the Secretary) to request his attendance.*

*Mr Beard reported that he had just seen Mr Horlock and he said that, having regard to the fact that the inquiry was a private one, and that his chief (meaning Sir Arthur Vicars) was not getting fair play, he respectfully declined to attend.*

Solicitor-general: Then we are to understand that Mr Horlock refuses to be examined?

Chairman: Yes; he has definitely refused.

Examination of Mr Francis Bennett Goldney, FSA

*Goldney confirmed that he was Mayor of Canterbury and had held the office of Athlone Pursuivant in the Office of Arms, Dublin Castle, since early in 1907. His first visit following his appointment by Lord Aberdeen had been in May 1907 when he stayed for three or four days as a guest of Sir Arthur Vicars. As a fellow member of the Society of Antiquaries, he had met Sir Arthur Vicars 'a good many years ago'.*

Solicitor-general: Now, you have told us that you only stayed in Dublin three days at the time you came on the opening of the Exhibition. Did you see the Crown Jewels when you came here?

Goldney: Yes.

Solicitor-general: Did any other people see them on that occasion?

Goldney: Yes; Lady Donegall and Lady Orford, and another lady, an American, a friend of Lady Donegall's. Sir Arthur Vicars asked them if they would like to see the State Rooms, and the other things in the Castle, and we went over the State Rooms; and when we came back Sir Arthur showed us the jewels.

Solicitor-general: In other words, Sir Arthur Vicars volunteered to those ladies to show them the jewels?

Goldney: I think what he volunteered to show them was the State Apartments. Whether they asked to see the jewels or not I do not know. I know they appeared to be greatly interested in what they saw. I remember Lady Orford saying she thought it a great pity that the jewels should be shut up in a place like this; and I remember Sir Arthur Vicars saying that before they were here in this part of the Castle they used to be kept in an old tin box in another place, and that the same care was not taken of them then as now. He said it was since his time the strongroom had been built to keep them in.

Solicitor-general: All this, I understand, was confidentially disclosed by Sir Arthur to those ladies?

Goldney: Well, I would not say it was confidentially disclosed, for I remember seeing some strange gentleman in the room, who came in to ask some question. I know there was some stranger in the room during part of the time, and I thought to myself whether it was well to be talking about the jewels in the presence of a stranger. I did not say anything, but the thing passed in my mind. It occurred to me that it was an imprudent thing – I would not say perhaps that it was imprudent – but that it was a curious thing to have such a conversation in a stranger's presence. I remember looking at him and wondering in my own mind what sort of person he was.

Solicitor-general: You thought it was a curious thing that those jewels should be shown to a person whom you thought was a stranger?

Goldney: Well, there was a low table between him and them, and I think he could hardly see them.

Solicitor-general: But this person was present on the occasion when Sir Arthur Vicars had this conversation that you have mentioned about the jewels?

Goldney: Yes; during part of the conversation.

Solicitor-General: Was he present during a portion of the time during which the jewels were being shown?

Goldney: He was. I do not remember his name at this moment.

Solicitor-general: When next did you see them?

Goldney: I saw them on the occasion I was here at the time of the opening of the Exhibition in May. In the State Room.

Solicitor-general: How did you come to see the jewels on that occasion?

Goldney: Lady Fairbairn asked Sir Arthur if he would show the jewels to a lady who was in Dublin. I do not know her name. I think she was a relative – a sister or a cousin of Lady Fairbairn, who was on a visit with her in Dublin. I remember the circumstance very well, because Sir Arthur kept us waiting for some considerable time.

Solicitor-general: Did you come back to Ireland at all after that?

Goldney: Yes; I came back on the occasion of the King's visit in July. I arrived on the Monday preceding his visit.

Solicitor-general: That was the Monday after the discovery of the robbery?

Goldney: Yes. I should not have come over so soon as the Monday but that I got a telegram from Sir Arthur Vicars to come at once.

Solicitor-general: On receiving that telegram from Sir Arthur Vicars you came over to Dublin at once? And you arrived on Monday morning, the 8th of July?

Goldney: Yes. I had intended to come over on the Monday, but I came on the Sunday in consequence of the urgent telegram I received.

Solicitor-general: And on your arrival you saw Sir Arthur Vicars. Can you charge your memory to repeat what he said?

Goldney: I cannot repeat his words; but he told me he had been to the safe, that the reason of his going to it was because a knight had recently died; and he told me that when he got to the safe the door was undone, and the jewels were gone.

Solicitor-general: What did you say?

Goldney: I expressed my surprise. I cannot give you the details of the conversation. It ended in my going to my own room and having a bath. I had only just arrived in Dublin.

Solicitor-general: At what hour did you arrive?

Goldney: I arrived at the house, I suppose, at about seven in the morning, and had had a very rough passage. After that, we came down here to the Castle, perhaps at about eleven o'clock.

Solicitor-general: Did you ask him what had been done about the jewels?

Goldney: I did. You are referring, I suppose, to the conversation that took place in his room upon my arrival, and I don't want to state anything that was not said during that conversation. Of course, I asked him a good deal about it, and he talked a great deal, but I find it difficult to remember exactly what he said.

Solicitor-general: Did he tell you, or did you know, that he, and he alone, had the key of the safe?

Goldney: I cannot say whether I asked him the question, or whether he told me so, in that conversation; but I know I learned that afterwards.

Solicitor-general: Can you say what explanation he gave you as to how the safe had been opened, he being the only person who had the key?

Goldney: No. He said he could not understand it; it was a mystery to him, he said.

Solicitor-general: Did he tell you on that occasion that the door of the strongroom had also been found open?

Goldney: No. I ascertained that afterwards. It was from one of the attendants here that I afterwards heard that.

Solicitor-general: Did you speak about that to Sir Arthur Vicars afterwards?

Goldney: I did. I said I had heard that the door of the strongroom had been found open, and he said it was; and I cannot recollect whether it was during the same conversation, or subsequently, he said he was so much bewildered, or flabbergasted, by what had occurred that he had forgotten to mention it previously.

Solicitor-general: State again, as accurately as you can, what you said to him, and what he said to you, about the strongroom door?

Goldney: I said I had been asking some questions in the office, and that I had been informed that the strongroom door had been found to have been opened on the Saturday night. He said that was so, and that he had quite forgotten to mention it.

Solicitor-general: Did you ask him how that could have occurred?

Goldney: Yes. He said he could not understand it at all. I think he told me there were two or three keys. I know he said there were two; and he may have said three. He said Stivey had one, and I think he mentioned the name of another official who had one. I know he said there were more than his own key.

Solicitor-general: Either then or at any other time did he give you any explanation of how he thought the door could have been opened?

Goldney: He said it must have been either with his own key or with a fabricated key.

Solicitor-general: Did he ever suggest to you any explanation of how the safe had been opened?

Goldney: No; except that someone had got a duplicate key, or a false key.

Solicitor-General: Did you ask him how he thought a key could have been fabricated?

Goldney: I asked him how he thought the key could have been copied. He said he did not know. I said: 'Do you think that anyone could have got the key out of your possession, and had it copied?' He said he did not understand how it could be done. I said I thought it was a highly improbable thing.

Solicitor-general: Did he mention to you that there was a second key of the safe?

Goldney: Yes; he told me he had a second key, and that he kept it in a place where no one could find it. ... He said it was in a drawer in his house at St James's Terrace. He also told me that he kept it in the centre of the drawer; that that was the safest place; because people when searching a drawer looked in the corners of the drawer and not at the centre; and that the centre was the safest place in which to put it. I asked him was it possible that anyone could have found the key in the drawer, and got a key fabricated from it. He said it was not possible. I asked him was it possible that the safe could have been left open. He said it was not possible; that he always, before leaving the office, went to the safe and made sure that it was locked.

Solicitor-general: Has it occurred to you as a possible explanation that when the safe was last opened it was left by carelessness unlocked?

Goldney: Yes. It is possible, but I think it is unlikely.

Solicitor-general: Do you not think that the opening of the strongroom door on Friday night had some relation to the robbery of the jewels?

Goldney: I cannot help thinking that it had; but I cannot be certain. I have thought over the matter a great many times, but I have not come to any conclusion. I still keep an open mind about it.

Chairman: It has been stated today that his (Sir Arthur Vicars') first idea was that it was the work of some of the swell mob who came over to Dublin on the occasion of the King's visit. Did he suggest that to you?

Goldney: Yes. I think we discussed that and every other possibility. After the King's visit I asked him to come and stay with me for a while at Canterbury, for he was very much run down in health. He came, and while he was with me on that visit we discussed every possible explanation we could think of. I suppose it was about August. He stayed with me on that visit, and I have not seen him since.

Chairman: We are in this position that we do not know what evidence you are prepared to give us. Have you any information you can give us on the subject of this inquiry? I do not mean any hypothesis; but has any fact come to your knowledge, as to which you have not been asked, bearing on the subject of our inquiry?

Solicitor-general: I am in the same position, sir; I have not been furnished with any statement as to the evidence the witness can give. I do not ask him to give us any hypothesis, but if he is aware of any facts, which, in his opinion, would throw a light upon the subject of the inquiry, I would ask him to state them.

Goldney: Well, sir, I am in this difficulty, that I do not know how much to say, or how little, or how far I would be justified in stating things that might only tend to raise suspicions. In fact, I do not suspect anybody as being guilty of taking the jewels. Whether, in my mind, I suspect that certain persons may know something about it is another matter.

Chairman: If any matter has come to your knowledge, which you think would give us any assistance on the subject of our inquiry, I will take it on myself, if you wish, to direct the shorthand writer not to take a note of it. Do you, Mr Solicitor-General, see any objection to our doing that?

Solicitor-general: I am entirely in the hands of the Commission, sir.

Chairman: [to the witness]: Is the difficulty you feel that you draw a distinction between what you would state at a public inquiry, and what you might feel at liberty to say to us in private?

Goldney: No, sir; the difficulty I feel is this: that if this was a public inquiry, and I was giving evidence on my oath, I would of course be bound to answer questions which, if put to me at the present investigation, I do not feel myself bound to answer, because I do not know whether I would be justified in doing so. [The witness then made a statement.]

Chairman: The statement you have just made does not refer to matters that have any bearing upon our inquiry, and I must direct the reporter to strike it out of his notes, as not relevant.

Goldney: Before I retire, sir, I wish to state with reference to Sir Arthur Vicars, that from my personal knowledge, in my opinion he was always fussily careful of the office.

### Examination of Mr F.J. O'Hare

*Mr F.J. O'Hare of Milner's Safe Company Ltd, 22 Dawson Street, Dublin, confirmed that he had been asked to attend the Office of Arms in the afternoon of Monday 8th July and made a thorough examination of the lock of the strongroom door in the presence of an officer.*

*He explained that he had examined the lock and taken it to pieces.*

*There were seven levers in the lock. Over a period of three and a half hours, he examined each piece of the lock minutely and exhaustively, and especially the appearance of the levers. If any attempt had been made to open the lock with a counterfeit or fabricated key, he said that the examination of the levers would have shown it.*

Solicitor-general: As the result of your examination, can you tell us, as an expert, whether that lock had been picked?

O'hare: No, sir. My examination showed, not only that it had not been picked, but also that no attempt had ever been made to pick it. If anyone had attempted to pick it, the attempt would have been visible. It was a high-class lock, and if any attempt had been made to pick it there would have been scratches on the levers, from the pressure on the levers in the process of picking, but the levers were perfectly clean and bright, without a vestige of a scratch.

Chairman: Suppose a fabricated key had been made, an exact imitation of the original key, could the lock have been opened with it?

O'hare: Yes, sir. Of course an exact reproduction of the original key would open it.

Chairman: Suppose a wax impression had been taken from the original key, and that a key had been made from the wax impression, would such a key as that show any signs if it had been used to open the lock?

O'hare: It would, sir. The difficulty would be to make an exact reproduction of the original key. With a lock of this kind, the key would require to be as carefully and exactly finished as the original key, which, in the process of wax reproduction, would be impossible. If such a key was used, though it might open the lock, there would still be some signs of pressure visible upon the levers.

Solicitor-general: Then your opinion is that it is practically impossible that the lock could have been opened by means of a key produced from a wax impression?

O'hare: Yes, sir.

Chairman: Does it not follow from that that it must have been opened with one of its own keys?

O'hare: Yes, sir; or with a reproduction made from it by a workman.

Examination of Mr Cornelius Gallagher

*Mr Cornelius Gallagher, an expert in the construction of safe locks, confirmed that he was employed by the Ratner Safe Company and had been called to the Office of Arms on Tuesday 9th July to examine the lock on the Ratner safe.*

*He explained that he had removed the lock from the door, taken all the levers out and examined every one. The whole examination took from two to three hours.*

Solicitor-general: Did you examine this lock, in order to see whether there was any mark or trace of its having been picked?

Gallagher: I did, sir, carefully. It was neither picked nor attempted to be picked.

Solicitor-general: Is it your conclusion that the lock must have been opened by its own key?

Gallagher: It must have been opened either by its own key, or with one similar to it, and it must have been made very like it, or there would have been a mark made on the lever. The key it was opened with must have been very nicely made, or it would have made a mark on the levers in some way, and there was no mark on any of the levers.

Solicitor-general: Then, in your opinion, it must either have been opened with its own key, or with a fabricated key made from the original key?

Gallagher: Yes, sir.

Solicitor-general: Of course you are aware that a key may be fabricated from a wax impression? Do you think that a key so fabricated could do it?

Gallagher: Well, sir, it might open the lock well enough, but it would leave some impression upon the levers. If you take an impression of a key in wax, there will always be some parts either smaller or larger, and you never can get a key so exactly made from it that it will not leave some mark on the levers when opening the lock with it. There was nothing of the kind.

Jones: How long would it take a skilful workman to make such a key, supposing he had the original before him? Could he do it in a day?

Gallagher: If I started to do it the day I got it I might do it, but it would take me some time.

Examination of Mr W.V. Harrel, MVO

*Harrel, Assistant Commissioner of the Dublin Metropolitan Police, first heard of the robbery of the jewels at 3 p.m. on Saturday 8th July, when he was told that Sir Arthur Vicars wanted to see him immediately in the Office of Arms.*

Solicitor-general: Were there any other persons in the room?

Harrel: Yes, Mr Burtchaell, Mr Horlock and Mr Mahony were

here, part of the time, also Superintendent Lowe. When I went into the room, Sir Arthur Vicars was standing beside the safe, and he said: 'The Crown Jewels are gone.'

I asked him how it had occurred, and he told me that Lord De Ros's collar had been returned that morning, and that he had sent Stivey down with it to put it in the safe, of which he gave him the key, that he himself had followed down almost immediately and that he found Stivey at the door of the safe, and that Stivey told him he could not open it, that he used some expression of surprise, and then he said that he tried the safe and found it open. That he examined the boxes, and he showed me how he had examined them, and that when he saw the key in the top box, which contained the jewels, he immediately felt that something was wrong, as he was in the habit of leaving the key in the second box; that on opening the top box he found the jewels were gone; that he then opened the boxes underneath, which contained the collars, and found the collars were gone and the boxes empty.

He told me that his mother's jewels had also been there; that they had recently come into his possession, and that they were gone. He said: 'This is the fault of the Board of Works, I asked them for a safe in the strongroom, and they did not give it; if they had given it this would not have happened.'

Solicitor-general: What did you say in reply to that?

Harrel: I was much struck by that statement, and said to him: 'Did you actually ask for a safe in the strongroom?' He said: 'Yes; I have the correspondence upstairs, and will show it to you.' I said: 'Don't mind that at present.' Superintendent Lowe then asked whether the door of the strongroom had been disturbed or bore the appearance of having been forced in any way. He said no. We then looked at the door of the safe; and I gave it a superficial examination and said it did not appear to have been forced he agreed with me – in fact he told me there were no marks on it. I, of course, could not see any, but I intended to get it examined by a specialist. I then asked him: 'When did you see the jewels last? When last did you show them to anybody?' He said: 'I am not sure whether I showed them to Dr Finney; but I believe I showed them to Mr Hodgson.' I asked him when; he said he was not quite sure but he got that visitors' book which is already in evidence, and I myself saw the entries in the book – Dr Finney, 26th June, and Mr Hodgson, 11th June. I said to Sir Arthur Vicars: 'You should wire at once to both those gentlemen, asking them whether they did see them, if you are unable to state it definitely.' 'Oh', said he, 'that would let everyone know about it.' I said: 'That does not necessarily follow, but it must be done, whether or not.' He seemed very much excited at the time, and still made some difficulty about it. I said: 'This must be done at once.' And Mr Burtchaell said: 'Why don't you do what Mr Harrel tells you?' He said: 'What can I say?' And he sat down to write the telegrams, but gave it up, and I then dictated the telegrams to him. One of them was to Dr Finney: 'Am anxious to know latest date on which safe with jewels was opened. Do you recollect whether I showed them to you when here, 26th June? Wire reply. Letter following.' And a similar one was sent to Mr Hodgson. Wires were received in reply from both. Dr Finney stated that he had not seen them. Mr Hodgson stated that he had.

Sir Arthur Vicars then said that he would explain how the thing occurred; and he opened the safe, and described the method of opening to me. I do not know whether it is necessary to give the description; it has been described already. I then told the Superintendent that I had to go down to my office, and told him to get from Sir Arthur Vicars an accurate list of the things that had been stolen. He did so, and here (producing large hand-bill) is a notice which we had printed, offering a reward of £1,000. This notice gives a full description of the articles.

Solicitor-general: On that Saturday, either in the office or else-where, did Sir Arthur Vicars inform you at all of the strongroom door having been found open in the morning?

Harrel: No. I did not know it till Monday morning.

Solicitor-general: Did you see Sir Arthur Vicars again on the Saturday?

Harrel: I did. I went to the Office of Arms again afterwards, and saw him. I went into the strongroom and looked at it. At that time I had no idea that anything had occurred in connection with the door of the strongroom, but he spoke about his key, and he showed me by demonstration how he kept the key of the strongroom on his chain, and he also showed me the key of the safe; that it was always on his bunch, and that the keys never left his possession.

I said: 'Now, is that really the case? It is not a thing that many people could say.' He said: 'Yes, it is; they have never left my possession; I have always been most careful.'

I then put a question to him. I said: 'For instance, on the occasion of a function at the Castle, when you are here in uniform, how do you carry that bunch of keys in your uniform?' He replied: 'Oh, well, on a night of that sort of course I put the keys in my overcoat pocket.' I said: 'And what do you do with the overcoat?' He said: 'I leave it in Herschell's room' – meaning Lord Herschell, the Private Secretary of the Lord Lieutenant.

In a subsequent statement, not made to me, he said that he had a special pocket made in his coat, and that the key of the safe was, on those nights, removed from his ring and kept in the pocket.

Chairman: Did he in any of those conversations express suspicion with regard to any particular person – I do not want you to name the person – but did he mention that he suspected anyone?

Harrel: Yes; he mentioned one person; but I may say, without mentioning the name, that after full inquiry we found there was no foundation for his suspicion. And I may add that Sir Arthur Vicars himself abandoned the suspicion altogether afterwards.

Solicitor-general: Now, Mr Harrel, I want to ask you a few questions arising on the statements (of Sir Arthur Vicars). First of all, there is mention made that Phillips, the coachman, had access to his keys. You have stated that Sir Arthur Vicars, in one of his conversations with you, mentioned that he had some suspicions with regard to a particular person – was Phillips the name of that person?

Harrel: Yes.

Solicitor-general: You stated that, after full inquiry, you found that there was no foundation for that suspicion. And that Sir Arthur Vicars himself afterwards abandoned the idea?

Harrel: Yes, entirely; there was really no foundation for it whatever.

Solicitor-general: (Reads the passage in Sir Arthur Vicars' statement as to his having shown the jewels to some lady friends.)

Beyond the statement that he had shown them to those ladies, between the months of March and June, did he ever state that he had shown them to any other persons?

Harrel: No; not till quite recently.

Solicitor-general: Have you since discovered, or did he inform you, that he also showed them to other persons – to Mr Esme Percy, and to Mrs Brown-Potter?

Harrel: Yes. That statement was made to me (by Sir Arthur Vicars) on the 12th of November.

Solicitor-general: Also to Miss Newman, a friend of Mr

Horlock's, between March and June?

Harrel: Yes; so I was informed.

Solicitor-general: Did you ever speak to Sir Arthur Vicars about his having shown them to Miss Newman?

Harrel: No. I wish to say, as regards Miss Newman, of course the police were not pursuing the inquiry on the same lines that this Commission are doing. Once we were satisfied that, in a criminal point of view, there was no reason for pursuing the investigation with regard to any person, it was dropped.

Starkie: I wish to ask you, Mr Solicitor-General, whether you suggest that Sir Arthur Vicars was wrong in showing the jewels to those persons?

Solicitor-general: Certainly, sir. He had no authority at all to show them to any person.

Harrel: I wish to mention one matter that I have omitted to state. I asked Sir Arthur Vicars whether it would be possible to identify the jewels if they were found. He said yes, it would. That he had inquired from a man at West's whether the jewels could be identified, and had been told that beyond question they could. That they were priceless stones, not at present in the market, and could be identified by experts.

Solicitor-general: I wish to ask you, Mr Harrel, did you speak to Sir Arthur Vicars on that Saturday about the second key of the safe?

Harrel: I did. He told me he had a second key for the safe, and that that key was in a drawer in a writing table in his own house. I said to him: 'Would you go and see whether that key is now there?' He said he had so much to do that he could not go then, but would go at the earliest moment possible – about seven o'clock. I asked him to let me know at once when he went home whether they key was there, and he said he would. And he telephoned to me that evening that the key was there, just as he had left it, and that he could see no trace of it having been tampered with.

Solicitor-general: Did you examine the place to see whether it showed any traces of forcible entry?

Harrel: Yes, and there were none. We made a most minute examination of the entire office from top to bottom. We left nothing undone in the way of examination, even to the taking down of a wall behind which there was a hollow space.

Solicitor-general: Would you explain to the Commission what system is adopted for guarding the Castle and the offices and the approaches to them?

Harrel: Yes. First, at the main gate, there is always a military guard both day and night, and there is always a sentry on duty, who walks up and down just outside the Office of Arms.

There are three other gates – the Main gate, the Lower Castle Yard gate, and the Ship Street gate. There is the military guard at the main gate, but at each of the other gates, and at the main gate only, there is a policeman on duty throughout the 24 hours every day. The military are responsible for the closing of the gates for wheeled traffic, which they do at sundown every evening. When that is done the gates are locked, and a constable has charge of the wicket gates. They are kept at night at all the gates; and, as regards the Ship Street gate it is closed entirely, and there is no traffic allowed at all.

During the day people may go through the Lower Castle Yard and out through the Ship Street gate, but at sundown the Ship Street gate is closed, and no one can pass. As I have stated, there is a policeman on duty at the gates by day and night; and I should mention that those men's duties are not defined as are the duties of a sentry. The police have a responsibility of their own; and they are most particular not to allow anyone to pass after dark without knowing what their business is; and they never leave their posts, because there is always another constable in the Upper and Lower Yards, and if the man at the gate has occasion for any reason to leave his post for a while, he must summon that other constable to take his place at the gate until he comes back; so that, as far as the police regulations can ensure it, no person can enter or leave the precincts of the Castle and the offices without being observed. There is no reason to think that anyone could enter the gates without being observed, and the police knowing all about them.

Solicitor-general: Assuming the outer door was shut on that night of July the 5th, it of course follows that the person who removed the jewels, if they were removed that night, must have used three keys, one for the outer door, one for the strongroom door and one for the safe?

Harrel: Yes; certainly.

Jones: Was inquiry made from the police on guard as to the people who came in or went out of the Castle Yard on that night?

Harrel: Yes; they were all strictly questioned; and I have statements here from the soldiers who were on duty there; and none of them saw anything in the least degree questionable.

Jones: Did any of the police tell you that they had seen Sir Arthur leave the Castle that night?

Harrel: No.

Jones: The last account we have of his movements that evening is his own statement that he left Mr Horlock outside the door of his own office, and went to the Chief Secretary's office.

Harrel: Yes.

Day Four: Tuesday 14th January 1908

Further examination of Mr F. Bennett Goldney

Chairman: Mr Solicitor-General, I understand that Mr Goldney wishes to supplement his evidence given yesterday by some explanation?

Goldney: Yes sir; if I may. First of all, I should like to say that I have not got the telegram with me that I spoke of – Ulster's telegram to me to come at once. I have several telegrams with me that say 'Come over at once' from Ulster, but they are not of that date. (Witness handed in the following telegrams.)

*22 October*

College Green, Dublin

To G, Hursley Park, Winchester.  Go and see Harry on way through London, and come over at once. Ulster

*23 October, Private*
West Strand Bennett-G, c/o Sir George Cooper, Hursley, Winchester .

Want see you urgently, come up please, wire me train. Vicars

*24 October*

West Strand

Bennett-G, Hursley Park, Hursley, Winchester Want see you urgently, come up please for couple hours, to show important document and consult with G.L. Very important and urgent. Vicars

*13 January*

Chapelizod

To G, Shelbourne Hotel Not without consent of Solicitors, Messrs Meredith [Unsigned]


Solicitor-general: Who was G.L.?

Goldney: Sir George Lewis.

Chairman: Had that important document any bearing upon this case, or was it private?

Goldney: Indirectly it had. I do not want to prejudice the case one way or the other, but since I knew, which was not for some time afterwards, that Sir Arthur Vicars had these obligations – and that I knew he was not well off from what he had told me, because he had told me of his joint expenses of his house – I urged him to go into a smaller house, and I said: 'At any rate you ought not to have any obligations which you cannot pay. It does not seem to me to be a right thing at all, and there has been considerable misunderstanding, and I am going to have my matter put in Lewis' hands. May I put yours right at the same time?'

He then told me, as I have told you before, that he had money difficulties. I said then: 'If you are in money difficulties I hope you will come to me, because I will certainly try and help you.'

That is what that refers to, and Sir George Lewis had both affairs put straight. And I signed bills, being told Sir Arthur Vicars wished me to do so, and that it was to a family solicitor. Afterwards I found that it was to a notorious moneylender, so that it was a matter that really required to be put straight at once.

Solicitor-general: What was the date of the bill you signed?

Goldney: It must have been, I suppose, in the spring of 1907.

Jones: Did you sign two on that date?

Goldney: I signed two at different times. It was under peculiar circumstances. I was away from home. I had been in Paris, and I arrived back, and my mother handed me a telegram saying, 'I am coming down by the eight train', from this gentleman. This was Saturday. He came and he said: 'I am in a great hole, I cannot go over to Ireland to see Sir Arthur Vicars, who has requested me to help him in this matter; it is merely a question of shares, and it must be done at once. I must have the money by Monday morning, and unless I can get somebody to do it I shall be in the greatest difficulty.' I demurred, and then he said: 'My family solicitor is coming down this evening', and then about half an hour afterwards, sure enough, a gentleman appeared with a black bag, and asked me if I knew what business he had come on, and I said: 'I presume you have come about this business.' And he said that he had, and he said: 'You are Mayor of Canterbury' and other things. I said: 'You must find that out from other people', or words to that effect. And he said: 'Are you prepared to sign this bill?' I said: 'I do not like it, but as it is to please Sir Arthur Vicars, and I am to be in his office, I will do it.'

Chairman: To please Sir Arthur Vicars you signed this bill for Shackleton?

Goldney: Yes, and I was told that it was his old family solicitor, and that the whole thing was to be put square, and that it was only for a week or less than a week. But it never was put straight, and there was a good deal of unpleasantness and difficulty about it.

Chairman: How much was that for?

Goldney: £1,500.

Chairman: You signed another?

Goldney: I signed a previous one – his cancelled it – almost under similar circumstances, and I did not take any more notice of it.

Jones: When did the £1,500 bill become due?

Goldney: It was to be paid back in some instalments, I think. I do not even know whether it was negotiated. I took the document and the letters about that bill to Sir George Lewis and asked him to see to the whole thing, and he did.

Chairman: Somebody must have paid the bill, Mr Goldney, if Shackleton did not?

Goldney: Oh, Sir George Lewis insisted upon it that it should be paid at once, because he was able to bring a certain amount of pressure, I suppose, and it was paid off. It was paid off, as a matter of fact, I believe, by Mr Shackleton's brother, but I do not know for certain, but they were both paid off together.

Jones: That was in October some time?

Goldney: Yes, but it was merely by chance that I happened to find out anything about it being wrong, and that the man was a moneylender. I was asked by a friend: 'Do you know the name of this family solicitor?' And I said: 'I do not think I do.' But I have a letter from this gentleman which, I understand, is exonerating me from having any responsibility.

Jones: Then did you sign a bill for Sir Arthur Vicars for £600?

Goldney: No; Sir Arthur Vicars signed for Shackleton. I have never lent Sir Arthur Vicars money in my life. I have offered to do so.

Chairman: The previous bill, was that also signed to please Sir Arthur Vicars?

Goldney: So I was told; I believed that it was so. It is just the same. There has been a little friction, I dare say you know of it, between members in the office owing to money, and it has always been over this question. I helped these people, honestly believing it was Sir Arthur Vicars' wish that I should do so, and it was merely by chance that I talked to Sir Arthur Vicars about money matters, and then he told me: 'I never asked you to do it, and never wished you even to do it, and did not even know all the details.' Then we began to compare notes, and I found out things that I had no idea of. I think that you ought to know that when I spoke to Sir Arthur Vicars, urging him to go into a smaller house, he told me that he had more than once asked to come and live here in this office, and that he thought that it would be much more desirable and everything would be so much safer. There had been some doubt about the office being left at night and nobody being here.

I do not think a doubt had crossed my mind that the jewels were unsafe because they were left at night, but I think you should know this, that after the jewels were stolen one of the members of the Office of Arms said to me that he had doubted whether they were safe or not.

Solicitor-general: Who had doubted?

Goldney: It was Mr Shackleton who spoke to Sir Arthur Vicars and me and said that he had told a lady only a few days before the robbery that he should never be surprised to wake up one morning and find them stolen. Sir Arthur Vicars was really annoyed at this statement, and he said: 'Well, if you thought they were unsafe why did not you ever speak of it to me?' I asked him: 'Why did you think they were unsafe, and why did you say such an extraordinary thing at such a peculiar time?' And he said: 'Because the office was left at night and because it was so lonely.'

The reason of his saying it was peculiar, but, I think, a perfectly straightforward one, but the reason it is impressed on my memory so well is this, that when he came over on the boat a lady with whom he had been at lunch only a few days previously said to him (I do not profess to give the exact words, but this is the exact meaning), she said to him: 'Oh, Mr Shackleton, what a curious thing that you should have been saying to us the other day that you should wake up one morning to find the jewels gone, and now we are reading in the paper that they are gone.'

Chairman: When Sir Arthur Vicars asked him 'Why did not you tell me', what answer did he make to that?

Goldney: I cannot remember what exact answer he did make. We had a good deal of it afterwards and Sir Arthur Vicars was quite angry about it.

Jones: Was this bill that Sir Arthur Vicars had signed for Shackleton in the hands of moneylenders, too?

Goldney: I cannot say; I think it was in the hands of these same people. But I do not think Sir Arthur Vicars had any more idea than I, or the man in the moon, that the people were money-lenders, and not his family solicitors. I have never seen that man that came down with this black bag from that day to this. But why I spoke of Sir Arthur Vicars' expenses in his house was that I might be able to say how it was that I had urged him to leave his house, and how it was that I said that he would like to come and live here, because he thought that if he lived here it would be more satisfactory altogether, because somebody would be sleeping on the premises.

Chairman: Have you any further statement to make?

Goldney: Yes; one. That I think the gentleman who was in the room when Lady Donegall was here was Lord Hawkesbury, the son of Lord Liverpool. I think it was Sir Arthur Vicars or it may have been Mr Burtchaell afterwards told me. You asked me yesterday who it was and I could not tell you at the time.

Chairman: The only thing that I want to ask you is, can you fix approximately the date at which Sir Arthur Vicars told you that it would be much safer if he were allowed to stay on the premises?

Goldney: He never said that it would be much safer for the jewels; he said it would be more satisfactory if somebody was sleeping on the premises, for the general safety of the place.

Solicitor-general: As I understand, Mr Shackleton came over in or about the time of the King's visit?

Goldney: Yes. I came over on the Sunday, and he followed either on Monday night or Tuesday night.

Solicitor-general: And therefore the conversation you have alluded to took place either at the breakfast on Tuesday 9th or on Wednesday 10th. Did you say that Sir Arthur Vicars was angry at the time?

Goldney: Yes, and he seemed very much upset about it afterwards, because in speaking to me afterwards he said: 'Why on earth, if he thought the jewels were unsafe, why could not he have said so, and then I should have been saved all this trouble.'

Solicitor-general: I observe that Sir Arthur Vicars' statement on the 12th of July, contains this passage: 'I do not suggest any single one of my staff had anything to do with it, nor do I suspect my maid-servant or footman, nor any person, who slept in my house.' He stated that on the 12th of July, after your departure?

Goldney: Yes.

Solicitor-general: And after that conversation that you have now spoken of by Shackleton?

Goldney: Yes. I do not think he did suspect anybody.

Solicitor-general: You have gone into this money matter which deals with Mr Shackleton in his absence, and have a certain reluctance to deal with it?

Goldney: Of course, you see how the money matter appears on the face of what I have to say. You see how the money matter relates to my conversation with Sir Arthur Vicars as to his leaving St James's Terrace, and of his telling me of his desire to come here.

Chairman: At the time of this conversation these two bills were still outstanding, and had not been settled, the £1,500, and the £600?

Goldney: No, they had not. I may say it is all settled now.

Solicitor-general: I have no desire to go very far into these money matters, but I understand you said that the result of pressure brought to bear, apparently in October 1907, was that the money was paid up?

Goldney: The money was paid up at that time owing to what Sir George Lewis wrote to Mr Shackleton.

Solicitor-general: And do I understand that the money was paid by Mr Shackleton's brother?

Goldney: That is my belief, but I cannot say.

Solicitor-general: Who is Mr Shackleton's brother?

*Although Goldney refrained from answering, Mr Shackleton's brother was, in fact, the famous explorer, Ernest, who in 1907 embarked for the first time as leader of an expedition to the region of the South Pole, and at the time of the incident of the loss of the Crown Jewels was seeking funds to finance the exploration.*

Solicitor-general: Now, I want to get this from you, when did you come to Dublin for this visit today?

Goldney: I left Canterbury on Sunday night.

Solicitor-general: Did you see Sir Arthur Vicars at all since you came this time?

Goldney: Yes, certainly, I met him by accident yesterday and there were other people present. I telegraphed in the morning to find out who was acting generally for the Officers of Arms; that is what I wanted to get at, because I am unrepresented by counsel at all, and I called on Mr Meredith in 32 Molesworth Street, but he was not in, and I waited, and at last Mr Meredith came along, and he said that it was not he who had charge of the case for Sir Arthur Vicars, but his brother, and if I would come back I should probably see him.

So when I left this office yesterday I went to 32 Molesworth Street, and Sir Arthur Vicars was in the room with the two Mr Merediths, and I did not see Sir Arthur Vicars alone. I asked to see Mr Meredith alone, which I did, and then Mr Meredith went out of the room and saw Sir Arthur Vicars, and brought me back a message and said Sir Arthur Vicars would like to offer me some hospitality, and I said that I would rather not, as I did not intend to call on Sir Arthur during my visit to Dublin, as I felt it would be better that I did not. I do not want you to think that I have been seeing Sir Arthur Vicars privately.

Solicitor-general: How did you go to see Mr Meredith yesterday?

Goldney: I saw in the newspaper that Mr Healy was counsel, and I telegraphed to Mr Healy, and he sent me Mr Meredith's address. When I left Canterbury I did not know what I might be wanted for here, and I did not know whether I ought to be represented by counsel or not, and my father, who is a barrister, said that the best thing that I could do was to see Mr Healy and ask if I ought to be represented by counsel. So I telegraphed to Healy in the morning, and he said: 'Not without consent of solicitors, Messrs Meredith.' So I looked into the directory, but I could not see him. He was not there.

Chairman: You did not see him till after you gave your evidence yesterday?

Goldney: No, because he was not there. I saw a lame gentleman, his brother, who said that he was very sorry his brother would not be there till eleven, and I said I must be at the Office of Arms at half past ten, and I did not know whether I ought to come here alone or not, you know. I wanted to know if I ought to have counsel representing me. I said to his brother that I would go back and see his brother afterwards, and I should like to see that I should have somebody to act for me in Dublin if it was necessary in future.

Solicitor-general: What occurred yesterday to make you desirous of having a solicitor to act for you in connection with this affair in Dublin?

Goldney: Well, nothing in particular, but do you not see this is a serious case?

Solicitor-general: That is, for you?

Goldney: No, but for Sir Arthur Vicars. And I do not know that I am not obliged to look into the future. I am not sure whether there may not be another commission, a public inquiry, and I think that it is desirable that a man who is not a solicitor or lawyer should be represented by counsel in serious affairs.

Chairman: I think it right to state, Mr Solicitor, that we thought it well, as so much evidence has been given before us that seems to affect Sir Arthur Vicars in his character as custodian of these jewels, to give him another opportunity of appearing here and explaining matters that we think require explanation, so by our direction this morning the Secretary has written to Messrs Meredith, informing them that evidence has been given here which seems to us to bear on the question of vigilance and care in the custody of the jewels, and that if he is willing to assist the Commissioners by giving them any explanation we shall be ready to hear him, and that he may be accompanied by his counsel.

### Further examination of Mr W.V. Harrel, MVO

*In continuance of Harrel's evidence, the Solicitor-General reminded him about the one of the four strong-room keys and one of the safe keys acquired by the police on Monday 8th July.*

Solicitor-general: Did you have careful inquiries made from every locksmith in Dublin … as regards each of those two keys?

Harrel: Yes. Those keys were exhibited to every locksmith in Dublin, and in every hardware shop where keys were known to be made, and these people were asked whether any such keys had been made by them, or whether any person had made inquiry as to the making of such key. The inquiry by the police lasted for some days, and I believe that they exhausted every person in Dublin who was known to the police in any way in that trade. None of them had been approached on the subject, or had made similar keys, or had been asked to do so. I also communicated with Messrs Ratner and Messrs Milner, and they had never been asked by any person to supply duplicates of the keys of the safe or the strong-room.

Jones: Has any inquiry been made with the object of tracing what Sir Arthur Vicars' movements were that night?

Harrel: Well, there was; yes. Of course the difficulty that I really have about these matters is that I do not wish to say anything that would be detailing the steps taken by the police, and the information in their possession, beyond what might be absolutely necessary to enable the Commission to arrive at a conclusion in respect of the terms of reference that have been made to them.

Chairman: My colleagues of the Commission think that we ought to retire to consider this question of whether any inquiry of this sort is within the scope of our Commission or not. [The Commissioners then consulted in private.]

I wish to say that we have carefully considered the question of what evidence we ought to take from Mr Harrel, or any other person representing the police, in regard to the movements of the officials or of any other person, who had access to this office on the day preceding the disappearance of the jewels, or rather the discovery of the disappearance of the jewels, and while we are extremely unwilling to embark on anything that could be construed into a criminal investigation, or an idea that we were a commission appointed to find out who was the author of this crime, we are of opinion that we are bound to investigate all the circumstances connected with the disappearance of the jewels, and that any evidence that can be given as to the movements of anyone who had access, or who could have had access to the jewels on the night preceding their disappearance is strictly relevant to our inquiry.

Solicitor-general: I may say, sir, that that absolutely coincides with my own view as to the scope of the inquiry, and if it stops short of that I do not think that it will be in any sense complete or satisfactory, and my own desire would be to submit to the Commission all the facts from which the Commission can then draw its own deductions as to the circumstances of the loss.

I have no doubt that the police will have to be very cautious in this matter lest the interests of justice should be prejudiced in any way in the case. But it occurs to me, subject to what Mr Harrel may say, that there may be no objection to stating all the facts within his knowledge either relative to the movements of any of the officials or any other person who had access to the premises at the same time.

Chairman: If the police, or those representing them, can at any time satisfy us that the answering of any question would in any way prevent them from further prosecuting their inquiries or interfere with the course of justice, of course we will not ask them.

Solicitor-general: May I ask, Mr Harrel, do you know now anything about the movements of Sir Arthur Vicars that night beyond his own statement that he parted with Horlock outside the office and went to the Chief Secretary's office to use the telephone?

Harrel: Nothing, except that I believe that subsequent inquiry showed that he arrived home. I do not know at what hour.

Solicitor-general: As regards any other official or any other person having access to the office, do you know anything beyond what has been already revealed in the course of this Commission?

Harrel: No.

Jones: I can hardly understand such a bald state of affairs as exists so long a time after the disappearance of the jewels, that the only thing that is known is that he went home that night. There must be something more known about him.

Chairman: Who was the officer who prosecuted the inquiries?

Harrel: Oh, a number of them were so engaged. Of course, I can have them later on. There were inquiries made at the time about all the officials in the office.

Jones: Speaking for myself, I shall be very dissatisfied if I do not have more information of the movements of these people. I cannot imagine the police not having made inquiries, or somebody else not making inquiries; and we should get the result of those inquiries.

Chairman: Mr Harrel intimates that he will produce the officers who made the inquiries, or at least some of them, who can give us relevant evidence.

Solicitor-general: Before we go to police witnesses perhaps the Commission will allow Mr Hodgson, who has come over, to be examined.

## Examination of Mr John Crawford Hodgson, FSA

*Mr Hodgson, a Fellow of the Society of Antiquaries and Librarian to the Duke of Northumberland, confirmed that he was in Ireland on Monday 10th June, having arrived in Dublin the previous Friday morning. On Monday 10th he dined at the residence of Mr Chamney of the Bank of Ireland, with whom he was staying. On that occasion he met for the first time Sir Arthur Vicars, a fellow guest.*

Solicitor-general: During the course of the evening did Sir Arthur Vicars give you any invitation in regard to the Office of Arms?

Hodgson: Yes, he did. I have done a great deal of genealogical work in my own part of the country, and that is the reason perhaps of Sir Arthur Vicars being asked to meet me, and it was the more welcome to me because he, through one or two strains of his ancestry, comes from my part of the country. He is descended from the Tyneside family of Hedley, and the Northumberland family of Shafto. He asked me, if I was staying in Dublin, to call and visit him at the Castle. It was arranged that I should call here upon him at half past twelve, and he would show me some of the records of his office.

Solicitor-general: Did you come next day in pursuance of that invitation?

Hodgson: I came at half past twelve and I saw Sir Arthur Vicars. He showed me one, two, or three or four rooms, among them this present room.

Solicitor-general: When you came into this room did you see the safe?

Hodgson: If I remember aright I saw a huge bench or desk in the centre of the room. And then before I left he opened that safe which stood in the recess.

Solicitor-general: When he opened it did he show you anything?

Hodgson: Yes. He took two cases out of the safe, one of which contained a collar and the other a jewel.

Solicitor-general: Describe the jewel that he showed you?

Hodgson: I do not know that I can. It looked to me almost a mass of brilliants and so forth, two or three inches wide. (The pictorial representation of the jewels in the placard offering a reward was shown to the witness who was asked if the jewels he had seen corresponded.) I think so; I do not know which it was.

Solicitor-general: Was it a splendid jewel?

Hodgson: It was a very splendid jewel; it was, even to the uninitiated, a very splendid jewel.

Solicitor-general: What did he say they were?

Hodgson: I understood that they belonged to the Knights of Saint Patrick and to the Lord Lieutenant. And I think they were displayed to me on a desk in that window (pointing to the window at the end of the room). I think there was a sloping desk.

Solicitor-general: As I gather from you, the exhibition of the jewels was a voluntary act on the part of Sir Arthur Vicars?

Hodgson: Oh, certainly. It was a matter in which I was not interested, but of course I was grateful for his attention, and gratified.

Solicitor-general: You some time after that got a telegram from Sir Arthur Vicars, I believe. Have you got that telegram?

Hodgson: I have. I ought also to say that I have Sir Arthur Vicars permission to produce the correspondence, and I have it all. The telegram from the Chief Secretary's office, Dublin Castle, was addressed to me at Alnwick, marked 'reply paid': Am anxious to know latest date on which safe with jewels was opened. Do you recollect whether I showed them to you when here on 10th June? Wire reply. Letter follows VICARS, Ulster.

I replied to the telegram that I saw the jewels on Tuesday 11th June.

Chairman: Have you got the letter that followed?

Hodgson: Yes, sir. I have two letters of that date. (Reads as follows)

*6th July 1907*

*Private*
Dear Mr Hodgson,

Many thanks for your prompt reply to my wire. A dreadful thing has happened. On going to the safe in our office today to lock up the late Lord de Ros's collar, which had just been returned to me, to my horror I found the contents of the safe had been rifled and the Crown Jewels removed from their case and five gold collars of the Order of Saint Patrick (valued at £280 apiece) removed from their cases, and alas! my brother's jewel box in which were my mother's diamonds gone, which he had asked me to keep for him in safe custody.

In fact the only things left were the empty cases, and my patent and my and my brother's wills. I wanted to tell the police the last time I knew the contents were safe and the only two people I could remember lately being in office to whom I might have shown them, and I thought I had to one or the other, was yourself and Dr Finney of Kingston-on-Thames. He is an old friend of mine. I therefore wired to you and him.

He was at office on 26th June, and you on the 10th, Monday. He replied that he had not been shown them, so it takes us back to nearly a month when I knew all was safe. You say in your wire, Tuesday 11th, but I think you must be mistaken, as we met at Chammey's on the Saturday, and you came in on Monday, and the office diary gives your name on Monday 10th. It is not of much importance, only a day.

The police are hard at it, and the hue-and-cry will be raised all over Europe, but for the present keep this to yourself, absolutely. It is awful for me, but what more could mortal do when a safe lock is picked, as appears to be the case, for no sign of tampering with safe or lock is visible. I must end to catch post. Any details you can remember will be valued as much as whether you recollect my putting all away and locking safe. It was found unlocked, but I can swear I locked it.

Yours sincerely, A. Vicars,

I replied to that at once, saying that I was confident that my date was correct, because I knew from my cash-book. Then, by a later post, another letter came, of the same date. (Reads letter.)

7 St James's Terrace Clonskea, Dublin

*6th July 1907*

Dear Mr Hodgson,

Since writing in a hurry to catch post I have looked up my own diary, and find that you are quite right in saying you called at office on Tuesday 11th June, for I find I dined with Chamney on the 10th, but my office messenger has put your name down in the call book at office on Monday.

The object in view is to fix date for the police, when I can state absolutely that all was secure. The safe is a fine one (Ratcliffe and Horner) and the key of it never left my possession. It was always a source of anxiety to me, having charge of things of such value and during the Castle season I had to take them to the Lord Lieutenant on full-dress nights, and again get them up and lock them up in the safe, often at 3 a.m., but the police were always about, and a detective patrolled through my office at night.

The safe, as you know, was just inside a window, outside which a sentry patrolled night and day, and the guardroom of the Castle was next my office. The lock must have been picked, or else a duplicate key got. The safe was supplied in 1893 by the Board of Works. What greater precautions could I have taken? I have had to write to my brother to tell him of our mother's diamonds having been taken, but in fact they made a clean sweep of Saint Patrick collars and all. My only hope is that the stones may be traced, as they were of the finest Brazilian stones of the finest water and size, and such as cannot be had now at any price, and would be sure to be spotted in the diamond market if they appear.

You can imagine how I feel, these things taken almost from under one's nose, in a royal palace, two or three yards from the guard. Please keep these details as private, as I understand the police wish it for the present. I am much obliged for your prompt reply to my wire.

Yours sincerely, Arthur Vicars, Ulster.

Their Majesties, as you know, are coming here on the 10th, and I am wondering whether this robbery can have been carried out by London experts in thievery, who always follow in the wake of royal visits.

### Examination of Superintendent John Lowe

*The Superintendent of the Detective Branch of the Dublin Metropolitan Police confirmed to the Solicitor-General that he heard about the robbery on the Saturday between three and four o'clock in the afternoon, when William Stivey, then the office messenger, came for him. He came at once to the library where he found Sir Arthur Vicars, Mr Mahony, Mr Burtchaell and Mr Horlock. He was the first police officer to arrive on the scene. Stivey went in with him.*

Solicitor-general: As soon as you entered this room did Sir Arthur Vicars address you?

Lowe: He was standing over at the safe here, and he raised his head and said: 'A burglary has been committed here right under your very nose.' I asked him what was robbed, and he said: 'The jewels have been stolen from this safe, also a number of other things, collars. In fact', he said, 'a clean sweep has been made of the safe.'

Solicitor-general: Did Sir Arthur Vicars also tell you that a case containing his mother's jewels had been taken?

Lowe: Yes; he said they had also been taken. He was unable to give any information of the nature of the contents of the case because he had not the key. His brother, Mr George Mahony, had the key of that.

Solicitor-general: Did he then tell you how the discovery came about?

Lowe: Yes. He said that he had sent the office messenger, Stivey, with a collar which had been returned, belonging to the late Lord de Ros; he gave it to him in his office upstairs and gave him the key of the safe, or that bunch which had the key of the safe, pointing out the key of the safe to him – and told him to bring it down and put it in the safe; and that Stivey came down, and he a moment later followed him, and that he came into this office. Stivey was still at the safe, and, addressing Sir Arthur, said: 'Sir Arthur, you must not have locked the safe.' He said that he went round to the safe and tried the lever; he drew the bolts and opened the safe himself; that Stivey explained to him the reason for the observation, that he found that he had left the safe unlocked, was that he could not get the key into the proper slot to open it, but that he was able to get it into the other slot, which showed that the safe was open.

Solicitor-general: Did you then see the case from which the jewels were taken?

Lowe: The case was shown to me then; in fact all the cases were taken out of the safe and shown to me, including the case in which the jewels were contained.

Solicitor-general: Did you observe whether there was anything left in the red morocco case which had contained the jewels?

Lowe: There was a ribbon, and Sir Arthur Vicars explained to me that it had been attached to a badge.

Solicitor-general: How did he tell you it had been attached?

Lowe: By a clasp fastened on with two small screws and run on to a hook on the badge. Then he explained that it was a matter of difficulty to detach the jewel from the ribbon, as the two small screws were very fine, and difficult to manipulate, and it took some time to take them away, and the ribbon would then require some coaxing to get it off the hook.

Solicitor-general: So whoever removed the jewel must have unscrewed this clasp and removed it from the jewel?

Lowe: That is what he stated.

Solicitor-general: Did he say whether or not he had on any previous occasion given that key to anybody?

Lowe: He said that was the first time he had ever given the key of that safe to anyone, and in reply to my question he said that there were two keys for the safe, one of which he had secreted at home in his secretaire, that no one knew anything about, and the other he had on his key ring, and that no one else ever had those keys; he always kept them in his own custody.

Solicitor-general: Did he say anything to you about being careful when locking the safe whenever he opened it?

Lowe: In the course of conversation he described what his practice was when he came in at night or whenever he had occasion to take the jewels out of the safe. He said that on each occasion of locking the safe after removing the key he invariably tried the lever outside it to see that it was locked.

Solicitor-general: That allusion to coming at night would have reference to the fact that during the Castle season it might be necessary for Sir Arthur Vicars to bring back the jewels late at night?

Lowe: That is so. I believe that is why he made the observation.

Solicitor-general: Did he say anything to you on that occasion about the Board of Works?

Lowe: Yes. He said: 'The Board of Works are to be blamed for all this. Some time ago I applied for a safe which would go inside the strongroom. This safe is too large to go through the door. Had it been inside, this thing could not have happened. The application was refused.' A little later, in the same connection he spoke of that safe. The name Ratner was on the front of it, and he said he did not know what degree of confidence to place in that manufacture. He did not know much about it but that it was supplied by the Board of Works, who generally did not supply the best material. Had it been a Milner or a Chubb he would have had confidence in it. He said the lock of the strong-room door was a Milner's lock, and that he had implicit confidence in it.

Solicitor-general: Now, when he made that reference to the strong-room door and the lock on it, did you put him any question?

Lowe: I asked him then whether the strong-room door showed any signs of having been tampered with. He said 'No'.

Solicitor-general: Did you on that Saturday hear anything about the strong-room door having been found open on that morning?

Lowe: No. The first time I heard that the strong-room door had been found open on the morning of the 6th was on Sunday evening, when inquiries had been made from the office cleaner who was the first to make a statement with regard to its having been found open.

Solicitor-general: Now, did you on that occasion make an examination of the safe itself to see if it bore traces of having been tampered with? And did it bear any such traces?

Lowe: No sign of having been tampered with that I could discover.

Solicitor-general: Did you see the outer door?

Lowe: Yes; I examined the outer door and the building generally. Well, I didn't examine the building that day, it had got too late to do so, but I examined it fully on Sunday.

Solicitor-general: Did you examine the outer door on the Saturday?

Lowe: Not the slightest sign of violence having been used to any door in the building was seen.

Solicitor-general: Was there any report made to you, or in your office, as far as you know, of the outer door having been found open on the morning of the 3rd July?

Lowe: No, there was no report made to the police anywhere. If such report had been made it should have come to me.

Solicitor-general: Now, did Sir Arthur Vicars make any suggestion to you as to whether it was a fabricated key that must have been used?

Lowe: He made several references. First he said that the thing must have been done by thieves over from London for the King's visit, which was then approaching. He subsequently said: 'Someone must have obtained an impression of my keys.'

Solicitor-general: Now, I want to ask you about the keys. Do you know of any police officer at all, except Detective Kerr, possessing a key of the outer door?

Lowe: No other police officer of any rank has a key for any door of the building except that Kerr has a key for the outer door.

Solicitor-general: We are anxious to know, and can you tell us as a fact anything about – shall I use the word – the movements of Sir Arthur Vicars on that afternoon, or on the night of Friday 5th July. Do you know anything about it as a fact?

Lowe: I can give you nothing very definite. The result of the inquiries that we made on that point left me with the belief on my mind that he visited the Kildare Street Club, and afterwards went home, probably within an hour from the time that he had left here, but we have nothing definite to fix it, and could not find anything definite. He had been in the habit of visiting the Club; consequently no notice was taken of his visit on any particular occasion, but that was what I learned, that it was believed that he had visited the Club.

Kones: How long would it take him to get from here to Kildare Street Club and then home?

Lowe: It would depend whether he drove to the Club and then walked. He could get to the Kildare Street Club probably in seven or eight minutes, and if he drove home he could drive probably in ten from there.

Chairman: Did you make any inquiry of the servants at Sir

Arthur Vicars' house?

Lowe: The statements have been taken, and the sergeant who took them can be produced.

Chairman: Have Sir Arthur Vicars' servants been summoned as witnesses?

Solicitor-general: I understand not. Having regard to Sir Arthur Vicars' own attitude in the matter it would not be quite fair, possibly, to people in that position.

(To witness) Could you tell us, as the result of your inquiries, whether the constables on duty can remember at all his having left the Castle that day?

Lowe: I can find no trace of Sir Arthur Vicars' leaving the Castle that day. I think I interviewed every man who had been on duty about the place, and none of them could tell me that he had seen Sir Arthur Vicars leaving that evening.

Solicitor-general: Now, did you get possession of a key of the strong-room from Sir Arthur Vicars?

Lowe: Yes. I got a key of the safe and a key of the strong-room. They came from Sir Arthur Vicars. I got a key of the outer door from Kerr, the detective officer.

Solicitor-general: Sir Arthur Vicars gave you the key of the safe?

Lowe: Yes; it was the key he had been carrying about. Subsequently, probably some days later, one morning he spoke to me outside here at the door and asked me to exchange keys with him and give him the key which he had been carrying and he gave me the key which he had, and which he had kept at home before that, and that is the key which I have at present.

Jones: Did he give any reason for that?

Lowe: Well, the only reason I understood was that it was in connection with clairvoyance.

Jones: I should like to ask you, Superintendent Lowe, did you assist in the search of these premises after the discovery of the loss of the jewels?

Lowe: No, sir. Chief Inspector Cummins and Detective Officer Kerr made that search.

Starkie: When did the police first know that the King was coming to Dublin?

Harrel: I may say that the possibility of the visit and the approximate date were known a considerable time before. I have reason to recollect that, inasmuch as it had leaked out owing to His Majesty having offered a cup to the stewards of Leopardstown Races. The fact was not supposed to be made public, but it got into the press, and that was the first intimation that was received of the approaching visit. It was in the press at the beginning of June, and I believe before June 11th.

Solicitor-general: The Chairman made a very important intimation this morning to the effect that having regard to the matters that up to this had transpired in the course of the inquiry, the Commission thought that a communication should be addressed to Sir Arthur Vicars requesting him to appear before the Commission in order that he might make a statement or give evidence touching the matters which, in the judgement of the Commission, affect him. The importance of that intimation, having regard to the attitude taken up by Sir Arthur Vicars in regard to this inquiry, is obvious. I understand that a communication has been already made, or will be at once made, to Sir Arthur Vicars' solicitors to that effect.

Chairman: It has been made.

Solicitor-general: I am not in a position to anticipate what the possible reply may be to that. It may be that Sir Arthur Vicars and his advisers will still think that the fact that the inquiry is not public, in the sense that the press are not admitted, would be an objection to their acceding to the request of the Commission that Sir Arthur Vicars should attend and give evidence.

I understand the view of the Commission to be that it is right and desirable that he should be given an opportunity of attending and giving such explanation as he can in reference to these matters. I desire on the part of the government to intimate to the Commission the government's view that not merely will they offer no objection, but that they are absolutely desirous that Sir Arthur Vicars should know that if he comes forward in reply to that requisition of the Commission to give evidence relating to the matters affecting him, the government would not merely offer no objection, but they are desirous and anxious that his evidence, if he so desires, should be given under circumstances of the widest possible publicity.

If it is his view that it is in his interest that the press should be present on such occasion, and on the occasion of the examination of the further witnesses whom he might present to the Commission, the government are perfectly prepared to acquiesce in that view, and I suggest that an intimation to that effect should be given to Sir Arthur Vicars. If the Commission should think well to adopt that course, I would suggest that the further proceedings should be reserved, possibly till the arrival of an answer from Sir Arthur Vicars or from his advisers to the requisition or communication which will be addressed to him and to them from the Commission. I do not know whether that course will be regarded as a good one by the Commission.

Chairman: I may say, Mr Solicitor, that we are all of opinion that it is a very proper step on the part of the government to suggest that Sir Arthur Vicars evidence might, if he so chooses, be given in public, and that the inquiry should henceforth proceed in public, if he thinks that it would be in his own interest. In reference to that I may say that my attention was called for the first time when I saw the print of the first day's proceedings in full this morning to the following passage:

Chairman: Are you applying now for a public inquiry, or are you not?

Campbell: I am not applying to you for a public inquiry, for I know you have no power to grant it.

If I had heard that observation made – for though it is on the shorthand writer's notes, it entirely escaped my notice – I would have at once called attention to it. I would have interrupted Mr Campbell at once, for we have full powers under our Commission to hold our inquiry in public or private at our discretion, and I never would have encouraged Mr Campbell in his application for a public inquiry if I had been of opinion, or if any of us had been of opinion, that we had no power to grant it. We were perfectly prepared to hear an application for a public inquiry and to consider it and determine it on its merits.

Solicitor-general: So I certainly understood.

Chairman: It was only when Mr Campbell objected, not merely to the inquiry being private, but to the terms of reference and to the powers of the Commission – which would remain the same whether the inquiry was public or private – it was only then I stated that there was no use in asking for a public inquiry if his objection went to the root of an inquiry at all under our Commission.

It is only because his statement that we had no power to grant a public inquiry appears uncontradicted on the minutes of evidence that I make this observation, and I think it is perfectly proper to add that as far as the evidence has gone I do not see that there was anything in the evidence, with perhaps one or two slight exceptions which could have been easily excluded, which might not have been fairly made public from the beginning.

Solicitor-general: Having regard to your intimation that you will again give an opportunity to Sir Arthur Vicars to appear, I may repeat that the government will offer no objection to either his statement or the statements of his witnesses being made in public to the Commission, and, in fact, they desire that the fullest publicity should be given.

Chairman: We entirely agree on that, and we shall ask our Secretary to intimate to Messrs Meredith that if Sir Arthur Vicars desires to give his evidence in public, I mean in the presence of the press, the Commission will have no objection.

Solicitor-general: And, of course, the meaning of that is that the further course of the inquiry should be in public?

Chairman: If we begin with a public inquiry we must go on with it. In the meantime, are there any other witnesses that you think we might take in the afternoon, awaiting the answer of Sir Arthur Vicars?

Solicitor-general: Having regard to this new development, I think the more convenient course would be to await the answer of Sir Arthur Vicars and his advisers to the communication which you are now about to make.

Chairman: Then, Mr Solicitor, we will adopt that suggestion, and adjourn till half past ten tomorrow morning.

Day Five: Wednesday 15th January 1908

Chairman: Having heard much evidence which seems to us, in the absence of explanation or answer, to affect seriously Sir Arthur Vicars in his conduct as custodian of the lost jewels we thought it right to give him another opportunity of giving evidence before us. We offered to hear his evidence in the presence of his own counsel, and either in public or in private as he himself should choose.

Sir Arthur Vicars has definitely declined to take advantage of the opportunity which is offered him, and we must, therefore, conclude this inquiry without hearing his own statement of the facts or his explanation of the facts deposed to by other witnesses. We wish to correct a misapprehension. The offer to take Sir Arthur Vicars' evidence in public was made before the receipt of the first letter from his solicitors in which he refused to appear before us.

There are one or two points upon which I myself wish to get some further information. The first point I wish to direct your attention to, and on which I think we ought to have some evidence, is as to the rule which you hinted at against Sir Arthur Vicars showing the jewels to anybody. I have not up to the present heard whether there is such a rule.

Solicitor-general. So far as I know, sir, there is no positive rule; the only rules dealing with the matter that I know of are the very Statutes themselves. There is no particular statute that I know of that authorizes him to show the jewels.

Chairman: But is there anything against his showing them?

Solicitor-general: No actual prohibition.

Chairman: Then another matter on which we ought to have some evidence is as to the allegation which was made by Sir

Arthur Vicars on several occasions that the circumstance that the safe was in this room and not in the strong-room was not his fault, but the fault of the Board of Works.

Solicitor-general: I will deal with that certainly.

## Further examination of Mr W.V. Harrel

Solicitor-general: The Commissioners were anxious to know the date on which it was known in Dublin that His Majesty was to visit Ireland in 1907?

Harrel: The *Dublin Daily Express* of Thursday 6th June contains the following:

Royal Visit – Date of Arrival of the King and Queen – Official Statement – Special Racing Fixture at Leopardstown – Arrangements for His Majesty's Visit.

We have received a communication from the Vice-Regal Lodge officially authorizing the announcement that His Majesty the King, accompanied by Queen Alexandra, will make a private visit to Ireland on 10th July, arriving at Kingstown in the Royal Yacht early on the morning of that day. Further arrangements will be announced in due course.

## Examination of Chief Inspector Richard Cummins

*Cummins informed the Solicitor-General that on Monday 8th July, at about 5 p.m., he and Detective Officer Kerr were instructed to make a search in the Office of Arms by Superintendent Lowe. An arrangement was made for the following morning, when Sir Arthur Vicars accompanied them in their search.*

Solicitor-general: Will you kindly inform the Commissioners what you did, without going into details?

Cummins: We commenced in the basement. In the coal cellar there was some coal, and we turned it over completely, and we turned over every lumber board and box that was in the basement, and every nook and crevice that we could possibly look at were searched, and we did the same in this room and all the rooms to the very top.

Solicitor-general: And did Sir Arthur Vicars himself go over the papers with you?

Cummins: Yes, sir.

Solicitor-general: And in the result nothing was found?

Cummins: No, sir.

Solicitor-general: In the course of this search did you observe in any part of the premises any indication of a forcible entry by burglars or any other persons?

Cummins: None whatever.

Solicitor-general: Do you remember Sir Arthur Vicars making any observation with regard to any press?

Cummins: He did, sir, when we arrived at that press marked 'R S'. Sir Arthur Vicars remarked, this is the last press I tried on Friday evening before leaving.

Starkie: Are there any drains on the premises in which anything could be concealed?

Cummins: No sir, not that I could see.

Chairman: You are quite satisfied that the missing jewels and other things were not in this office?

Cummins: Quite satisfied, sir.

Examination of Detective Sergeant Patrick Murphy

*Murphy confirmed that he came to the Office of Arms immediately he was informed about 6 o'clock on Saturday that the state jewels had been stolen. Sir Arthur Vicars showed him, Superintendent Lowe and Sergeant Sheehan the safe from which the jewels had been abstracted.*

Solicitor-general: What statement did he make to you as to when he left the office on the preceding evening?

Murphy: He said to me that he left the office about ten minutes past seven, that he had let Stivey, the messenger, away some time before that, and that he came down stairs in company with Mr Horlock, and that he (Sir Arthur Vicars) remarked to Horlock: 'I will go my usual rounds of inspection.'

He stated that he passed through this library here, closing all the presses that were not closed, and went to the strongroom and tried the handle to see that it was locked, and found it all right.

Solicitor-general: Did he give you particulars of the various articles of jewellery that had been taken?

Murphy: He did, sir; he enumerated the various articles of jewellery that had been taken.

Solicitor-general: Did he express to you any opinion at that time as to how the robbery had taken place?

Murphy: He did, sir; in the course of conversation with me he stated that he believed that it had been done by what he called 'crack London burglars'.

Solicitor-general: On that occasion when you were here did he say anything at all about the strongroom door having been found open that morning?

Murphy: No, sir.

Solicitor-general: Did you afterwards ask Stivey why he did not mention the matter to you?

Murphy: I asked Stivey on the following Monday or Tuesday morning why it was that he did not make it known to us here on the Saturday that the strong-room door was found open. I mentioned to him that I had been with him on the Saturday, and that he had not told us about it. He said that as he had told Sir Arthur Vicars, and as Sir Arthur Vicars was present, he thought his duty was done when he had informed Sir Arthur Vicars about the matter.

Solicitor-general: When first, if at all, did you make an examination, you yourself, of the strongroom?

Murphy: I made an examination of the strongroom on the morning of the 16th July. In the presence of Stivey.

Solicitor-general: On that occasion did Stivey make any statement to you about the keys of the strong-room?

Murphy: He said there was only one key of the strong-room kept concealed in a drawer in the press in the strong-room, and that he thought or supposed that there was another kept in the box that was upstairs in Sir Arthur Vicars' office.

Solicitor-general: Did he tell you then who else had keys of the strong-room?

Murphy: He said Sir Arthur Vicars had a key, he himself had a key, Mr Mahony had a key which he had given up, and Mr Burtchaell formerly had a key, which he gave up about 12 months previous to that.

Solicitor-general: Now, did you on the 19th July see Sir Arthur Vicars about the keys of the strong-room?

Murphy: Yes, I saw him on the 18th or 19th of July.

Solicitor-general: What did he tell you?

Murphy: He told me that he had a key, that Stivey had a key, that Mr Mahony had a key which he had given up, that Mr Burtchaell had a key which he gave up about 12 months previous to that, and that these were the only four keys for the strong-room.

Solicitor-general: On that occasion when you were speaking to Sir Arthur Vicars did he tell you, so far as your memory serves, when it was that Mr Mahony gave him up his key of the strongroom?

Murphy: Not exactly at the time, but it was said after the robbery.

Solicitor-general: Now, do you remember examining the presses in the strong-room?

Murphy: I do, sir. On the 16th July.

Solicitor-general: Did you examine the glass case?

Murphy: Yes, it was the glass case I went there to examine. The press is the glass case where there is the Sword of State.

Solicitor-general: Did you, previous to your examination of the glass case, hear Sir Arthur Vicars make any statement about the glass?

Murphy: I did. He said that the burglars who took the jewels out of the safe in the library were afraid to take the jewels out of the glass case in the strong-room, because the glass was so thick and strong that the crash would be so loud that it would be heard outside, and they would likely get caught.

Solicitor-general: What was the date on which he made that statement about burglars?

Murphy: It would be probably about the 12th or 13th July.

Solicitor-general: Did you examine the glass?

Murphy: Yes, sir. Stivey opened the glass case, and I took a penny out of my pocket and put it inside of the glass and got my fingers outside in order to test the thickness of the glass. It did not appear to be nearly so strong as what Sir Arthur Vicars represented. I expected to find it thick plate glass.

Solicitor-general: I must ask you some questions to get the facts on the notes. The glass case you speak of within the strong-room is placed up against the partition wall dividing it from the messenger's room, is not that so?

Murphy: Yes, sir. Near the door as you turn inside.

Solicitor-general: Is there a window in the strong-room looking out into an area?

Murphy: There is, sir. It is secured at night by a sheet-iron shutter on the inside.

Solicitor-general: Are there bars upon the strong-room window?
murphy: I do not know that.

Solicitor-general: You have told us that the strong-room looks out into the area?

Murphy: Yes, sir.

Solicitor-general: And there are premises then abutting on the area?

Murphy: Yes, sir, the premises are used as a veterinary department and other departments belonging to the Castle.

Solicitor-general: But does anybody occupy them as a residence? Does anyone sleep in them at night?

Murphy: No, sir.

Solicitor-general: Did you on one occasion go with Sir Arthur Vicars to a place called Mulhuddart?

Murphy: I did sir, and Clonsilla, on the 15th July. Sir Arthur Vicars made some communication to the police, and I was directed to wait on Sir Arthur Vicars here, and to act under his instruction or at his suggestion. Mr Mahony was also with us.

Solicitor-general: Did Sir Arthur Vicars tell you what you were going there for?

Murphy: Yes; to search for the jewels in consequence of a statement that had been made to him by a clairvoyant at his residence in Saint James's Terrace on the previous Sunday.

Solicitor-general: Did you go to the churchyard?

Murphy: We did, sir; we searched Clonsilla and Mulhuddart churchyards. The clairvoyant had said that the jewels were concealed near a tombstone not far from the entrance of an old, disused churchyard in the direction of Clonsilla. Yes; we all three made a very vigilant search to see if there was any fresh earth or anything like that, and found nothing.

### Re-examination of Detective Officer Owen Kerr

Solicitor-general: Were you speaking to Sir Arthur Vicars on Monday 8th July about the robbery of the jewels?

Kerr: I was. He rested his two elbows on the big desk that stood here in this place, and he said: 'I would not be a bit surprised that they – the jewels – would be returned to my house by Parcel Post tomorrow morning. His Excellency, this evening, said the same thing.' I may remark that it was then between seven and eight o'clock in the evening, and I understood that there would be difficulty in sending by Parcel Post.

Solicitor-general: (To the Chairman) A statement was made, and as no one's name is mentioned in it I think it is only right, as Sir Arthur Vicars is not present, that the statement should be put in.

(To witness) On the 20th September were you in Sir Arthur Vicars' office, this office, again?

Kerr: I was, sir.

Solicitor-general: What was the first thing he said?

Kerr: He said to Stivey: 'Does Kerr want to see me?' I said: 'No, Sir Arthur.' And I came out there at the lower entrance door to where he was, near the door leading into the basement, and he said: 'If that door (pointing to it) had been locked it would never have occurred.'

Chairman: That is the door leading to the basement?

Kerr: Yes, sir. Sir Arthur Vicars proceeded to say, addressing me: 'They were taken by a man whom you know well. He was a guest in my house, and he treacherously took impressions of my keys when I was in my bath. He often came to this office for his letters on Sunday, and he used my latchkey to get in. He is in Paris at this moment, and here is a cipher telegram (displaying a tissue) that I am after receiving about him.'

Chairman: Did he say anything as to whether the jewels were disposed of, or would be disposed of ?

Kerr: He said: 'They are now a white elephant on his hands, and they will be returned.'

Jones: Do you know to whom he referred?

Kerr: To my mind it only referred to one individual. It would only fit into and answer the description of Mr Shackleton, because any persons that had a right to go into the place on a Sunday for letters were on the premises at the time, and he was the only gentleman who was absent.

Jones: Did he indicate to you when he thought it was done?

Kerr: He said it was done the Sunday after the King's visit. I mean the Sunday after the King's birthday.

Chairman: Sunday would be the 30th June. Did he explain to you why the robbery could not have been done if the door to the basement had been locked?

Kerr: I understood him to suggest that someone would have got in and been concealed in the cellar, and I said would it not be an absurd thing to think that anyone could come in here during the day and a messenger continually on duty, even supposing that he could expect to escape.

Chairman: Did you form any theory of your own as to what connection that had with the door to the basement being locked?

Kerr: I did, sir. From the remark that I then passed: 'Cannot it be definitely fixed whether that gentleman was in Ireland on that Sunday.' He said: 'He could be in Ireland, he could be in Dublin, and nothing known about it. Could not he have been staying on the North Wall.' As regards letting him in with the key on Sunday it conveyed to my mind that it was not on that particular Sunday that he got in with his latchkey to get his letters, but that he often came to this office on Sunday for his correspondence.

Chairman: But on this particular occasion he did not get the latchkey?

Kerr: He did not get the latchkey, and was not known to be in Ireland.

Solicitor-general: Did Sir Arthur Vicars tell you that he was not in Ireland so far as he knew on that occasion?

Kerr: No, sir; but I said could not it be definitely fixed whether that gentleman – without mentioning the name – was in Ireland or in Dublin on the Sunday, and his reply was: 'He could have been in Ireland; he could have been in Dublin, staying on the North Wall, without it being known.'

Solicitor-general: Did you ask him why he fixed the Sunday after the King's birthday?

Kerr: I did not. It was speculating. He spoke in a speculative tone.

Solicitor-general: Did you ask him how the supposition of his having come in on that Sunday after the King's birthday explained the strong-room being found open or the safe being open?

Kerr: On that occasion I did not, but I often asked him that question.

Chairman: I suppose it was that this man, being in Dublin, had got himself concealed somewhere in the basement? And that he had come up after the offices were closed and taken away the jewels?

Kerr: That was what it conveyed to my mind.

Chairman: And that if this door had been locked he could not have got in?

Kerr: Yes, and I said at the time that it seemed ridiculous that any outsider could come in during office hours when a messenger is continually on duty, because I often come in on messages from time to time during office hours and without ringing the bell, and I never could get inside the door without someone coming to ask me what I wanted. I said if he had no difficulty in getting impressions of his other keys, how much easier would it be for him to have got a latchkey, and that it seemed an unnecessary thing for him to come in in office hours when he would have so little difficulty in coming in after office hours.

Solicitor-general: I think it is right to put a question to you as you stated in reply to one of the Commissioners that, in your mind, in Sir Arthur Vicars' statement one particular gentleman was pointed out. And you have told the Commissioners, I understand, his name, and now it is only just to that gentleman I think to ask you this question. Do you know, as a matter of fact, when that gentleman whom you have indicated was last in Dublin prior to the discovery of the robbery?

Kerr: I do not, sir, but he made a statement to some of our officers fixing his movements before that. I don't know what steps were taken to corroborate his statement.

Starkie: Do you know that he was here in May?

Kerr: I do not know any particular day or week or month that he was here. His visits to this office were so few that I did not fix any particular time, and if I did see him coming in it would not leave such an impression on me, because I would regard it as legitimate.

Solicitor-general: (To the Chairman) That is the only evidence that I can give you on that question now. Mr Shackleton will be here tomorrow. Mr Burtchaell told us that he left Ireland in the early part of June. I thought it was right, having regard to the fact that Sir Arthur Vicars was not here, that the statement should be proved by this witness, and that he should have the full benefit of it.

Chairman: Certainly, and I think as far as possible we ought to have other statements made by Sir Arthur Vicars as he is not here to give us his own statement.

Examination of Colonel Sir John Ross of Bladensburg, KCB

*The Chief Commissioner of the Dublin Metropolitan Police confirmed that he met with Sir Arthur Vicars in the Library on July 6th, the day of the discovery, about 4 p.m.*

Solicitor-general: Where was he, and what did he say?

Ross: Well, directly he saw me he told me what had happened, and described it as we have already heard. He was standing at the safe, and I asked him to let me see it. He opened the safe, or at all events, he put his hand in and showed me the boxes, and he drew out a red leather case and said that the key was in the lock contrary to his usual custom of leaving the key outside, hanging from the box.

And then he opened the case, and I saw a blue ribbon in it. I said: 'Oh! They have left this blue ribbon behind.' And he said, 'Oh, yes, they have'. I said, 'Let me see it', and I looked at it because I had known that this blue ribbon had an ornament fastened to it. I thought that I should have seen it cut. I said to him: 'I suppose this is cut?' And he said 'No', and then he opened the ribbon out. I then saw a little eyelet-hole uncut, and he told me that the jewel was fastened on the ribbon and went, or a portion of it, went through this little eyelet-hole.

He said that it took a great deal of time to adjust the ornament on the ribbon or to take it off, and I then saw that it must have been done very deliberately, and that whoever did take the ornament must have taken time about it. I then asked him to show me the other cases.

Solicitor-general: Did he at all convey to you at that time that the ribbon had been attached to the jewel?

Ross: Well, I understood that at the time, and after a few days, as I will tell you by and by, I went up to ask him again on that point so as to be quite certain of it. It occurred to me at the moment that if the ornament had been fastened in such a way as to take some time to take it off or put it on, this time had been expended by the thief. Then I asked him to show me some of the collar boxes, and they were all empty. Most of the collars had been in cases of their own, and they could have been easily abstracted by being taken out. There was one box, however, that was merely a deal box, and Sir Arthur Vicars told me that in that box had been a collar which had belonged to the late Lord Cork, and at the death of Lord Cork the collar had been returned, not in its own case but in a deal box, and that the collar was wrapped up in silver paper. Sir Arthur Vicars told me that the paper with which the collar had been carefully surrounded was left and the collar gone. So it gave me the impression that there had been great deliberation in the removal of these things.

Solicitor-general: The paper had been carefully unwrapped?

Ross: The paper had been carefully unwrapped and left behind in the box and this struck me very much. But either on the Monday or the Tuesday – I think it was Tuesday 9th – I went to Sir Arthur Vicars and I said to him: 'I want particularly to ask you whether you are sure that the Lord Lieutenant's jewel was on the ribbon when you last put it away.' He told me he was quite certain that it was on the ribbon.

(The safe was here opened by Superintendent Lowe, who was called in, and the red morocco case taken out and submitted to the Commissioners.)

Solicitor-general: That is the case you are speaking of?

Ross: I think it is. It seems to be a little larger than what I remember, but I have no doubt that it is the same case. It contains a slip of paper with these words on it: 'Ribbon taken by me for Scotland Yard. A.V., Ulr. 3rd August 1907. Replaced 16th September 1907.'

Solicitor-general: Can you tell whether that is Sir Arthur Vicars' writing or not?

Ross: Well, it looks very like it. Oh, yes, I am sure it is. There is no doubt of that being Sir Arthur Vicars' writing.

Chairman: The ribbon was not wrapped up when you first saw it?

Ross: No; it was lying across, and the thing interested me. I took it and said: 'I suppose this is cut.'

Chairman: To what part of it is the jewels attached?

Ross: I do not know, for I have never seen how it is fastened. All I can say is what was said at the time, to explain that it was a very complicated affair. Sir Arthur Vicars said it took time to put it on and it took time to take it off, and I remember that when I looked at this I thought I should have seen it cut across, but it was not. My recollection of it was that when I saw it in July it had a little slot hole there.

Chairman: Did he tell you whether it was his habit to keep the key attached to this box?

Ross: Yes, I think he did. My recollection of it is this: he was describing what had happened when he made the discovery, and he said that his attention had been called to the red box having the key in the lock instead of its hanging down as it usually did, and then that full of fear and anxiety he had taken hold of the box and to his dismay he found the box was lighter than it ought to have been, and then that he opened it and found that it was empty.

Solicitor-general: Did you, on the Monday, ask Sir Arthur Vicars why nothing was said about the strongroom being open on the Saturday?

Ross: Yes, I asked him on Monday the 8th. He told me that he was so upset that he had forgotten it.

Examination of Chief Inspector John Kane

*Chief Inspector Kane of Scotland Yard confirmed that he arrived in Dublin on Thursday 11th July and came to see Sir Arthur Vicars in the Office of Arms. Sir Arthur Vicars showed him and Mr Lowe the red morocco case that had contained the jewels. The* solicitor-general *asked him what he observed when Sir Arthur Vicars opened the case.*

Kane: There was a small ribbon, I recollect distinctly, because he had previously described the ribbon before we had come to the safe, and had said that the thief could have been in no hurry at the safe, as the manipulation of the ribbon would have taken very considerable time to remove the ornament attached to it.

Then, on going to the safe, he produced the ribbon and manipulated it with his fingers showing the length of time that it would take to unscrew the jewel. My recollection is that there was a frayed portion of the ribbon on one side, and he showed how difficult it would be for an amateur, or for any person not acquainted with regalia, to shift the ornament over that frayed portion of the ribbon, and he was doing this in order to satisfy me that the thief had been in no hurry.

Jones: Apparently he satisfied you that the thief must have known all about it?

Kane: It satisfied me that the thief was in no hurry to leave the premises.

Chairman: And that he knew how to work it?

Kane: Oh, certainly. And you will appreciate, of course, that I am only stating facts that came under my observation, and I express no opinion whatever. I merely say what came under my observation for what it is worth.

The position was described to me first by Mr Lowe, and then, on seeing Sir Arthur Vicars in his room upstairs, I told him I would prefer to take it first hand from himself, as I had only had it from my colleague if I may so describe Mr Lowe. I said I would prefer to take it from him, so he went through the whole history of the case, and as soon as he had done I said: 'If my opinion is worth anything, Sir Arthur Vicars, at all, this gentleman (meaning Mr Lowe), must remain to look for the thief in this building, because what he had described to me would be utterly impossible, to my mind, on the part of an ordinary or outside thief.'

So then Sir Arthur Vicars took me down to the safe and showed it to me. He had already given a description of the trouble that the thief must have taken with that ribbon, and then he gave me an illustration of how the thing might be done.

Solicitor-general: Did he give you an account upstairs of how the ribbon had been attached?

Kane: Oh, yes, he did, and that was one of the items in the account which made me make the observation that I have just told you that no outside thief had done this thing, because the whole thing seemed to me so grotesque that an outside thief who had secured his booty would be so particular about the manipulation of the ribbon. And there were other points. All the cases from which those regalia and collars had been taken had been carefully restored to their original position. Experience teaches that when a thief secures his booty in another man's house, the first thing uppermost in his mind is to secure his retreat. What does he care whether cases are restored or collars in their boxes? He wants to get away.

Solicitor-general: You then came down here to the safe?

Kane: Yes; I had already heard about the strong-room door, and I had expressed an opinion on the strong-room as well.

Solicitor-general: Tell us what he said about the strong-room?

Kane: I asked him to give me his theory of the robbery and he told me first of all that some persons must have secured impressions of his keys and by this means obtained access to the building and then to the strong-room and the safe.

Of course I was aware at that time that the expert who had examined the locks had expressed his opinion that no false key had ever been used, and that he had given his reasons. Of course I had heard such reasons many times before, and I told Sir Arthur Vicars that it seemed improbable that forged keys were used at all.

Solicitor-general: What did he say to that?

Kane: I described to him why I thought so. I said, first of all, that if the thief came in predetermined to rob the strong-room he would have done so because he had opened it; and before he had forged the key for the strong-room he must have made up his mind to rob it otherwise one could not see any object in his forging the key of the strong-room at all, for the mere curiosity of opening it and looking at the articles there.

I said it was clear that the strong-room door was opened, and we must reasonably assume that whoever opened it went inside, 'and then', I said, 'if an outside thief did that will you please suggest why he did not secure some of the property there, such as the gold crown and the collection of valuable articles up on the shelf of an ordinary press, with ordinary glass in it, and I understand that even the key of the press was kept in a drawer of the table, in the middle of the room.'

He said: 'He was disturbed; he must have been disturbed.' I said: 'By whom or by what? You will recollect', I said, 'the leisurely way in which he operated at the safe. There was no hurry there. Put all these things before you – that he had operated at the safe first of all, and there was no hurry there. He was in the seclusion of a small strong-room at the back of a large and unoccupied house. What disturbed him? If disturbed, who chased him? Where did he go? How did he disappear? Has anybody picked up any of the stolen property that he dropped in his flight?' 'No, no', he said, 'I cannot account for that at all.'

'Then reverse the position', I said. 'Suppose he went to the strong-room first and that he were disturbed; do you suggest that after that he came here to rob the safe?' He could give no explanation. It was perfectly clear, I said, to my mind, that the man who did that has a knowledge of this building … and has more right on these premises than I have. I think those were the exact words that I used at the moment. This was all upstairs and then we came down and had a look at the safe.

Solicitor-general: Is that the ribbon? (Red morocco case with blue ribbon inside produced, and inspected by witness.)

Kane: In my opinion this is the ribbon I saw. I recollect it was something like that ribbon. Sir Arthur Vicars explained how difficult it would be, that it would take some time to work, I think the word he used was to 'coax', over this portion of the ribbon the actual ornament itself. More difficult to take it off than if the ribbon were quite new, but I could not understand how an outside thief would want to take it off at all instead of rolling it up and putting it in his pocket.

Chairman: Have you any theory as to why an inside thief should wish to take it off?

Kane: Well, the only theory I have is that this theft was not committed on the 5th of July. We will assume that some person conversant with the place – I am not making a suggestion against any person, I have no right to express an opinion at all about persons, I can only state facts – my theory is that he would be a person who would have time to remove it and would remove it at his leisure. It would be useless to an ordinary thief or housebreaker, or burglar coming in, to take that trouble. To me it is incomprehensible that any ordinary burglar should do so.

You might say that the burglar would not want to run any risk, but I may suggest, with great respect, that the burglar would run as great a risk of being caught with the diamonds alone as with the ribbon attached. I do not see why the burglar should want to detach it. He would roll it up and put it in his pocket, and clear off as quickly as possible. And the same observation I put to Sir Arthur Vicars.

Solicitor-general: Might it not happen that it might have been left in the hope that at some time the jewel might be restored by a person who took it for a temporary purpose?

Kane: Well, that suggestion will hardly apply to an outside thief.

Chairman: Had Sir Arthur Vicars suggested to you that it was burglars?

Kane: Oh, yes, because he was very emphatic in saying, when I insisted on pressing my view that it was some person acquainted with the building, 'I have implicit confidence in every member of my staff', and he repeated that over and over again.

Chairman: Did he ever, at any of your subsequent interviews, withdraw that theory?

Kane: He did. He accepted my view absolutely, that it was some person acquainted with the office. ... That would be after, I think, about the 2nd of August.

Starkie: Did he, at that time, implicate any person?

Kane: He did, sir. He mentioned the name of a person. (The witness paused.)

Solicitor-general: Having regard to the fact that it has been already mentioned in reply to the Commission, I do not think there is any harm in mentioning it now.

Kane: Am I directed to mention it? Personally I have no objection because it is common talk in London, in clubs, and other places, that he has accused this person. Mr Shackleton, Frank Richard Shackleton. Mr Shackleton is quite aware of it.

Solicitor-general: Did he tell you when last Shackleton was in Dublin to his knowledge?

Kane: Yes. I think he said about the 7th of June.

Solicitor-general: Did you ever put it to him how, if Shackleton was last in Dublin on the 7th of June, and that the jewels were seen in this office by Mr Hodgson, of Northumberland, on the 11th of June, Shackleton could have taken them?

Kane: Oh, yes, I put that to him several times, because I was, aware, of course, that the gentleman from Alnwick saw them on the 11th of June. I put that to him several times, and then he suggested that Shackleton was in collusion with other persons in this robbery.

Starkie: Did he convey to you whether the robbery took place on the night of the 5th of July or on some previous date?

Kane: He fixed it absolutely for the night of the 5th. That is where we could not agree, because I asked him: 'Do you associate the opening of the strong-room door with the robbery from the safe?' And he said, 'Unquestionably'.

Chairman: And you did not think that the robbery of the jewels and the opening of the strong-room door took place on the same night?

Kane: No; I did not.

Solicitor-general: On what did you form that opinion?

Kane: There I must object to expressing an opinion. I shall express no opinion, because if I expressed an opinion, that would lead up possibly to the involving of persons, and that I must not do. It would be the natural consequence, if I was to express an opinion, that I should have to explain how I associated the opening of the strong-room door that night with the robbery, but my opinion is that the robbery did not take place that night.

Starkie: Do you believe that the opening of the strong-room door was to account for the disappearance of the jewels?

Kane: I believe that whoever opened it – I make no suggestion in any shape or form – but the theory I formed at the time and the theory I maintain up to the present moment was that the strong-room door was purposely opened that night for the purpose of bringing about an investigation that would lead to the discovery of a robbery that had taken place before Friday night, the 5th of July. That impression I formed at the time and that impression I still maintain.

Starkie: Were you told of the incident of the finding of the hall door unlocked on the morning of the 3rd of July?

Kane: I was. To my mind the same object was intended to be achieved on the night of the 3rd which was intended on the 5th. We know that the persons who found those doors open did not do what one would have expected they would have done, rush off to the police at once and report it.

Chairman: I would just like to ask you another question. Why do you think that the person who opened the front door or the strongroom door wished to precipitate an investigation, have you formed any theory on that point?

Kane: Yes; I have. I have formed an opinion and I expressed it at the time. That there was a certain high personage coming here, and possibly certain people thought that when these jewels had disappeared it would be necessary that some explanation of that should be forthcoming before their arrival.

Chairman: But how was the thief interested in that?

Kane: That was just the very thing that I objected to at first, expressing an opinion about this matter at all, because it leads from one thing on to another. This will all possibly appear in Blue Book form and, therefore, I want to be very guarded. Besides I am not here under the protection of my superiors. I am certain that my superiors would, in the most positive terms, object to my expressing an opinion. A police officer has no right to express an opinion at all with regard to persons. I must only state facts.

Starkie: Did Sir Arthur Vicars give you any idea as to how an impression might have been taken of his keys?

Kane: Yes, he said it might have been done. I am speaking of the first occasion here when he was convinced that an impression had been taken. He said he had implicit confidence in his own staff and that he could not point to any person who could have had that opportunity. Many persons could have had it, but he could not particularise.

Solicitor-general: Did he ever on any occasion – I ask you in the widest sense – down to the present moment make any statement to you suggesting how any human being could have had an opportunity of getting possession of his keys?

Kane: No; he has never given me anything approaching a clue to how any outside person could have done that.

Starkie: Have you formed an opinion as to whether that safe there was locked or not from the date of the robbery up to the night of the 5th?

Kane: No; I have not formed an opinion about that, but I pointed out at the safe to Sir Arthur Vicars that it seemed to me so utterly impossible that any outside thief would have done all these things, putting back the cases, and I particularly noticed that this is a very large safe and I said: 'Just imagine an outside thief doing the very thing that might attract the attention of the sentry outside by closing a door which is very thick, in this front room, by shutting-to a strong-room door in the silence of the night.' I said he would have gone off and left the cases on the floor and the door wide open. And I specified the shutting of the door and the turning of the handle downwards, giving to the observer the appearance of a locked safe. I said an outside thief never did that.

Starkie: But if the jewels were taken for a temporary purpose and the safe left unlocked, anyone who turned the handle would discover that the jewels were gone and the thief would have no opportunity of returning them undiscovered?

Kane: Yes; if it was left open for some time; but in my mind the safe was unlocked the same night as the strong-room door.

Solicitor-general: Although it is your impression that the jewels had been taken on a prior occasion?

Kane: Oh, yes, because I cannot understand opening the strongroom door and touching nothing at all, because before the key was made, if an outsider did it, there must have been a predetermination to rob the strong-room, otherwise there is no sense in forging the key.

Solicitor-general: There is one matter I wish to ask you. Sir Arthur Vicars was in London, I understand, in the early part of August?

Kane: I saw him here about the 1st or 2nd of August.

Solicitor-general: Can you tell us whether he was continuously in London for a number of weeks in August and September?

Kane: He was, and used to stay with Mr Bennett Goldney and others, and used to come up to town.

Solicitor-general: Did he ever, on any one of those occasions give you any clue at all to how any person could have got possession of his keys?

Kane: No; he never gave me any explanation. Of course, at that time he had only one person in his mind.

Examination of Sir George C.V. Holmes KCVO, CB

*Sir George Holmes, chairman of the Board of Works since 15th April 1901, said that he remembered the transfer of the Office of Arms from the*

*Lower Castle Yard to the present office and was concerned with the readjustment of the new office for the reception of the Office of Arms. He confirmed that Sir Arthur Vicars had seen and approved the plans.*

Solicitor-general: Now, before I come in detail to that, do you remember when the safe in this present office, this one here, was first supplied to Sir Arthur Vicars?

Holmes: I can only tell you from information I have received. It was long before my time. It was 14 years ago. Before I was a member of the Board.

Solicitor-general: Now, at the time that this office was being readjusted for the reception of Sir Arthur Vicars, and the strong-room was being built, were you informed at all that it was his intention to place the safe containing the regalia in the strong-room?

Holmes: No, not during the time that the alterations were being made.

Solicitor-general: Had you yourself any knowledge at all of the obligation placed on Sir Arthur Vicars by the Statutes of the Order of Saint Patrick as to the custody of the jewels?

Holmes: None whatever.

Solicitor-general: And it follows from that that you did not know where, by the statutes, he was commanded to deposit the jewels?

Holmes: Certainly not.

Solicitor-general: Now, in 1903 the office was readjusted?

Holmes: It was in 1902 that the works were commenced.

Solicitor-general: When first was it that you heard that there was any question of a safe being placed in the strong-room?

Holmes: After the completion of the strong-room. The first information that reached me was in a letter from Sir Arthur Vicars himself of 25th April 1903.

Solicitor-general: And the proposal was that the existing safe should be exchanged for a narrower one, which could be put into the strong-room. What did you do on that?

Holmes: Well, the purchase of a new safe would have involved considerable expenditure of public money, and the existing safe was a burglar-proof and fire-proof article of the best possible construction. I was advised that the locks could not be picked, if at all, under 30 hours hard work and under what I may call favourable circumstances. Moreover, the safe was to be placed in a position where it would be under constant surveillance, that is to say, there would be a sentry always outside and a policeman always in front and it seemed to me, therefore, that it would be a waste of money to supply a new safe.

I sent for an officer of the Board of Works and directed him to ascertain if the existing safe could not by any possibility be put into the strong-room. He informed me, after inspecting the premises that it could, at the cost of a few pounds, be put through the window of the strong-room. It would be necessary to remove the bars for the time being and to replace them. I directed him to inform Sir Arthur Vicars of that and he reported to me shortly afterwards that he had done so. I cannot tell you the exact date.

I met Sir Arthur Vicars at the Kildare Street Club, and he at once began to speak to me about this very question. He said that he had been considering my offer to put the safe into the strong-room and had come to the conclusion that it was not necessary because the safe was burglar-proof and fire-proof, and the lock could not be picked in any time during which the office was not open to inspection. He added that there was a sentry behind and a policeman in front.

These were the very considerations which had occurred to me before; and then he said that he had come to the conclusion that he would be content with the safe for the present, if I would promise to exchange it at some future date whenever we could dispose of it elsewhere. I said that I would do that, and so the matter was dropped.

In December of that year the estimates for the Office of Arms for the next financial year came before me, and they included amongst other things a requisition from Ulster for a new safe which would go into the strong-room. He had told me, I should tell you, at the Kildare Street Club, that it was his intention to send a formal requisition for this safe, and as soon as I saw the requisition I entered a minute on the book.

Solicitor-general: Now, in the year 1904, I suppose you repeatedly saw Sir Arthur Vicars? Did he ever make any further requisition to you about the safe?

Holmes: No.

Solicitor-general: Did you ever, from that date up to the discovery of the robbery, hear a single thing in connection with the safe?

Holmes: Not a word.

Solicitor-general: Did he tell you, at any time after the Statutes of 1905 were framed, that the duty was thrown on him of placing the jewels in a steel safe in the strong-room?

Holmes: No.

Solicitor-general: Sir Arthur Vicars states that it was not till the strong-room was nearly complete, and the door fixed, that he discovered that the door was not wide enough to admit the safe, although he had all along pointed out that he wanted the safe to be placed inside. Did he ever point out to you, while the strong-room was being built, that he wanted the safe to be placed inside?

Holmes: No.

Solicitor-general: He says in his letter of the 13th July: 'I remember, and my letters bear it out, my asking for a Bramah lock'?

Holmes: That was for the strong-room door.

Solicitor-general: Was that the only reference ever made to a Bramah lock?

Holmes: As far as I know.

Solicitor-general: And did he refer to the safe?

Holmes: Oh, no; the safe was all right, and had been for many years provided with its lock. He had asked for a Milner's burglar-proof, not fireproof, safe for Crown Jewels. Milner's do not fit Bramah locks to their safes.

Solicitor-general: And you say that on that you made the entry that you have told us and under the conditions that you have told us?

Holmes: Yes.

Solicitor-general: Your understanding with Sir Arthur Vicars was that when on a future occasion you wanted the safe for another office you would exchange this one for a new one to be given to him?

Holmes: Yes.

Solicitor-general: We know how many keys of the safe there were. Have you anything to indicate officially how the keys of the safe came into the possession of Sir Arthur Vicars?

Holmes: Yes. There is a letter from the safe-maker. The letter says: 'The keys of this safe were sent from here by registered post direct to Mr Vicars on the 15th April, 1895.'

Solicitor-general: Do you know how many keys originally there were for the strong-room door?

Holmes: Two.

Solicitor-general: Had you anything to do with the supply of the third and fourth keys?

Holmes: No.

Solicitor-general: There is one matter that I wish to mention in connection with the previous statutes dealing with the duty of depositing the insignia. The obligation was this: in the Statutes of Lord Whitworth, who was Lord Lieutenant in 1814, it is stated that:

We are also pleased to direct and command that an iron chest, with a sufficient lock, shall be supplied to the said Ulster King of Arms or his deputy, and fixed in a safe room of the Office of Arms, in which such collars and objects shall be deposited for safe keeping until they be disposed of by the Grand Master …

and so forth. There is no reference, I understand, to the insignia at all. My own impression is that the insignia were not in existence then. Certainly they did not attach to the office of Lord Lieutenant and, therefore, they are not mentioned at all in this statute, and so far as I can discover there is no statute between then and 1905 which expressly mentions insignia belonging to the Lord Lieutenant.

Starkie: Was the Lord Lieutenant not Grand Master of the Order at the time?

Solicitor-general: He was, but I do not think the insignia existed.

Chairman: That is, the insignia which consists of the Lord Lieutenant's jewel?

Solicitor-general: The words in the statutes are 'collars and badges'. The statutes only deal with the collars and badges and not with the jewels, and it does not appear to be known when these regalia came into existence or were first placed in the custody of Ulster. All we know of them, so far as express statute goes, is that they were dealt with by the statutes of 1905, those that I have already referred to. Of course in that the obligation was distinct, namely, to place them in a steel safe in the strongroom.

Day 6: Thursday 16th January 1908

Solicitor-general: Yesterday I gave evidence, you will remember, concerning a certain statement made by Sir Arthur Vicars which implicated a particular person who was afterwards named in response to a question. I stated at that time that it was only fair to Sir Arthur Vicars that that evidence should be given, as he has not thought well to attend, so that his version of the case as affecting that person should be before the Commission.

Immediately after that I became acquainted with the fact that Sir Arthur Vicars had made a similar statement to another police officer, and I think that, before the person referred to is examined – and I understand he is in attendance to give his evidence before the Commission – it is only just that I should also present that information to the Commission, so that they may be apprised of it before they hear him.

Examination of Detective Sergeant Sheehan

Solicitor-general: On the 18th September, I believe, you had an interview with Sir Arthur Vicars in the Office of Arms?

Sheehan: Yes, sir; on that occasion he said that he would not be at all surprised if the jewels were returned to him by Parcel Post either at his residence or to the Office of Arms.

solicitor-general: Did he express any belief as to how the jewels were stolen?

Sheehan: He said that he believed the jewels were stolen by Shackleton; that Shackleton could have got a wax impression of his keys without much trouble; that he always left the keys in a bunch on his dressing-table when he was taking a bath; that he thought Shackleton also knew that he kept the key of the safe under his pillow in the bed, and that he could also take an impression of that.

Solicitor-general: When he spoke of the key that he kept under his pillow, was that the key of the safe or of the strong-room?

Sheehan: The key of the safe was under his pillow, and the key of the strong-room was on the bunch of keys which he left on the dressing-table while he was taking his bath.

Solicitor-general: Did he say anything at all to you on that occasion about the second key of the safe, which we understand he kept in his own house?

Sheehan: He did, sir; and on the 20th of September I had another interview with him in the office upstairs. He then told me that on the 28th June, the King's birthday, he had occasion to go to the office here to open letters, as the office was closed, and that when leaving his house he could not find the key of the hall-door of the office. That he came and got Detective Officer Kerr to open the door for him with his key; that he did not find his own key till some time in July, a day or so after Shackleton returned to his house, and that he then found it in its usual place on the dressing-table.

Solicitor-general: Now I want to put this to you, did he tell you when first it was that he came to suspect Shackleton?

Sheehan: He told me that he suspected Shackleton about a fortnight after the robbery being discovered; that Mr M'Ennery, of Dunboyne, visited him at the office here and told him (Sir Arthur Vicars) that he was almost certain that the jewels were stolen by Shackleton; that Shackleton was a shady customer in every respect.

Solicitor-general: Do I understand that he conveyed to you that his suspicion of Shackleton arose as the result of that statement of M'Ennery?

Sheehan: Yes, sir; he said that was the first time he suspected Shackleton.

Solicitor-general: There is only one other matter I want to ask. In Sir Arthur Vicars' statement of the 12th July 1907, he states that Mr M'Ennery, junior, of Rooskey House, Dunboyne, stayed in his house for one night, on the 2nd July. Do you know as a matter of fact whether that is the same Mr M'Ennery to whose statement he referred in his conversation with you?

Sheehan: Yes, sir; I believe so.

Jones: When you went to search the house, as you told us on the first occasion, didn't he show you the place where the second key of the safe was kept?

Sheehan: He did, sir. It was in a bookcase; it was concealed a foot or a foot-and-a-half down in the press, under old books and leaves of papers; he said that it was there he kept the key. It was locked up.

Jones: Did he say anything as to whether Shackleton knew where that key was kept?

Sheehan: He said nobody could know where that key was kept, only himself.

Chairman: Did you ever hear of Mr M'Ennery previous to this conversation?

Sheehan: No, sir, I heard nothing about him till I took that statement.

Solicitor-general: That, to my knowledge, gentlemen, was the first occasion on which this gentleman, Mr M'Ennery, was mentioned in any statement made by Sir Arthur Vicars except in his own statement of the 12th July, where he spoke of him as having slept in his house on the 2nd July, but in consequence of the statement made to the Commission I ascertained that a communication was made by Mr M'Ennery to Mr Harrel, and if it is desired by the Commission, Mr Harrel will attend to give evidence.

Chairman: If Mr M'Ennery knew any facts, that is, apart from suspicion, I think he ought to be a witness here, but if he did not know any facts I don't see what use his evidence would be at all.

Solicitor-general: That's precisely the impression I am under. As I understand, he was absolutely ignorant of the facts, but lest there should be any question about it hereafter I have not the least objection to the statement being got from Mr Harrel, or to Mr M'Ennery being called, but beyond mere statements and suggestions, I understand he never conveyed any facts to the police.

Chairman: I gather from Sergeant Sheehan's own statement about what Sir Arthur Vicars said, that it was merely speculation on the part of Mr M'Ennery arising out of some previous knowledge he had of Shackleton's character, and I don't think that would be evidence in any way.

### Examination of Mr Francis Richard Shackleton

Solicitor-general: Except in the case of this gentleman and in the case of Mr Goldney, I had a general idea of the facts that were within the knowledge of every particular witness when he came forward, and on that account, with your permission, you may remember, I stated the more convenient course was that I should put questions for the purpose of eliciting the facts; but on the present occasion, in dealing with this gentleman, I am not in possession of the facts within his knowledge, and I think that, having regard to all the circumstances of the case, the more convenient and proper course would be that he should, at least in the first instance, state to the Commission what he knows concerning this matter. I take it that the Commission would afterwards allow me to ask him any question that might occur to me for the purpose of developing that information.

Chairman: Of course, if you do not know what his evidence is.

Solicitor-general: He did make a statement to the police; on 12th July he made certain statements to the police to which I may afterwards refer.

*Shackleton informed the Chairman that he first became connected with this office in about October 1899, when he was appointed Assistant Secretary to the Office of Arms by Sir Arthur Vicars.*

*Prior to that Shackleton's acquaintance with Sir Arthur was mainly through correspondence on heraldic matters and genealogy. Shackleton explained that he had been trying to get into the Heralds' College in England and that it was gradually suggested that he might come on as unpaid secretary in order to learn as much as possible.*

*Shackleton came over to Dublin in October 1889, first staying in rooms and then from May 1990 living in barracks in Dublin as an officer in the 3rd Battalion Royal Irish Fusiliers, Armagh Militia. During this period he was 'going back and forwards' to the Office of Arms in the afternoons.*

*In January 1901 he went out to South Africa on special service. On being invalided out in September 1901 he moved to Devonshire and did not resume work in the Office of Arms.*

*He could not remember when he first came back to Dublin but knew he was there for the King's visit in 1903, when he was Gold Staff officer.*

Chairman: How long did you remain at that time?

Shackleton: Well, I rather feel it was only a matter of a few days, but I could not say distinctly now. It was a short time, certainly, and what makes me think it was short is that I remember getting a telegram.

Chairman: After that, when was your next visit to Ireland?

Shackleton: I do not remember at all. I am sure I must have been backwards and forwards. I have been travelling for three days and three nights, and am rather tired.

Chairman: Do you remember when the Office of Arms was transferred to this building?

Shackleton: I think it was very much about that time, about the date of the King's visit, sometime in 1903, I think. I know the King's visit was when the office was in the Lower Castle Yard. I remember using the back staircase, the private staircase to the State apartments, in and out at intervals, and seeing him daily.

Chairman: When you came back did you find the offices removed to this building?

Shackleton: On one occasion of my returning to Dublin I found that during my absence the transfer of this office had taken place, but whether it was immediately after the King's visit I cannot remember.

Chairman: Can you tell us at what date you took up your residence in St James's Terrace with Sir Arthur Vicars?

Shackleton: The house was taken in July or August 1905. I do not think the move was made till September or the end of August, when I came for, I think, two days, and the house was not ready. It might have been for a week. I do not remember. I do not suppose that I spent more than about two months and two weeks during the whole two years all put together. I think I was up to a fortnight there during the last year.

Chairman: What was the arrangement between you and Sir Arthur Vicars?

Shackleton: The arrangement between Sir Arthur Vicars and myself was this: I paid half the rent, rates and taxes, half the servants' wages, board and ordinary wages, half the washing of all the household things, everything in the house with the exception of Sir Arthur Vicars' personal washing; that is to say the clothes that he wore. The sheets and everything like that also went into my bill. I paid half the coal bill and half the food for the period that I was in the house. The servants were on board wages, but when I came to stop in the house the arrangement was that I should pay half the food of the period, and to make certain that I was not using separate food that had been bought the day before I arrived, I always counted half of the day previous to my arrival, allowing for the day after I left. I paid for the whole of the upkeep of the gardens, and the planting and laying out. I paid for half of all the repairs in the house and alterations of grates, and things like that. And I took the half of everything.

Chairman: That seems to have been a very favourable arrangement at any rate for Sir Arthur Vicars. You say you occupied the place for about two months?

Shackleton: I may be wrong. It may be three months in the first year, but it was not more than a fortnight in the second year. I do not think it was three months in the first.

Chairman: While you were living in the house you were well acquainted with Sir Arthur Vicars' habits … how he kept his belongings?

Shackleton: Yes, I was well acquainted with them.

Chairman: Had you a key for the door of the office?

Shackleton: No, I only got, twice in my life, the key of the door of the office, that is when Sir Arthur Vicars let me go in on a Sunday to get my own letters in 1906-1907.

Chairman: Had you ever a key of the strong-room or of the safe?

Shackleton: Never.

Chairman: Had you ever a latchkey of the outer door, or a key of the strong-room, or a key of the safe at any time in your possession?

Shackleton: Never of strong-room or the safe. I never had a key of the outer door except, perhaps, on a Sunday, when I came in for important letters from London. I might have had it on a Bank Holiday, when Sir Arthur Vicars wanted me to go in and get letters, and I used to drop the key into the letterbox when I left. It might have been the office messenger's key I had, not Sir Arthur Vicars'. I am not quite clear on that point.

Chairman: Would it be true if it were suggested that at any time you had a latchkey of the outer door in your possession for several weeks?

Shackleton: From the night of Saturday to the morning of Sunday, when I came for letters – that, I should say, would be the longest period.

Chairman: How often would you come to the office while you were residing in Dublin?

Shackleton: Every day if I were residing in Dublin.

Chairman: When you came here you found the outer door open?

Shackleton: Well, occasionally I have had to wait a few minutes because the cleaner had gone and the office messenger had not arrived, and occasionally I had to wait on the doorstep, because

I was always the first of the officials to arrive.

Chairman: Had you ever occasion to go to the strong-room while you were working in the office?

Shackleton: Frequently. The strong-room was always open the whole day long, more or less, with the exception of the periods when the office messenger went out.

Chairman: And what about the grill?

Shackleton: If the grill was not wide open – of course it constitutes portion of the strong-room, which was always open – the key would be hanging in the grill, which is as good as calling it always open. I had absolute access to it even when the messenger was out. All I had to do was to go to the drawer in the table just outside here where the office messenger sat and take the key from the drawer, and open the strong-room and go in.

Chairman: And had you ever access to the safe?

Shackleton: Never. I thought, on one occasion that I had charge of the key of the safe, and I was in great terror, because when he was away once I had the key of the key box, I thought that a key in the small key box – it was not a key box, it was a black despatch box – this was in the Lower Castle Yard, and in that box were kept various papers, confirmations waiting to be finished, things like that, and the office keys. There were keys which I thought were the keys of the safe in that box. I had been given the key of the despatch box to hold so as to be able to open the presses when we were in the Lower Castle Yard, and at the time I imagined that the key of the safe was there, but I am told it was not.

Chairman: Do you mean that the key of the despatch box also opened the presses?

Shackleton: No. The keys were contained in the box, the key of which box I had whole days in my charge together, and I wore it on a piece of string around my neck because I believed at the time that some of the keys on the bunch contained in the box, the key of which I had, were two keys of the safe; but I am told they were never in that box. I want to convey that I did think that I had charge of the safe key once, and I said so to Sir Arthur Vicars, and he said: 'No, you never had charge.' I said: 'Were not they in that box when I had the key of it?' He said: 'Never. You might have thought that they were, but never.' I did not know the key of the safe at that time.

Chairman: Now I am going to ask you some questions which I only ask you in consequence of statements which were made here, and you need not answer them unless you like. Were you in monetary difficulties in 1907?

Shackleton: Yes. Well, I had been for two years, I may say, in difficulties; that is to say my difficulties could easily have been relieved had I chosen to go to my family and tell them; but for various reasons I did not care to do so, and I borrowed money, not from my banker, but from a moneylender. You may ask any question you like, but I understood it was merely in relation to Sir Arthur Vicars and the custody of the keys that I was to come here. But I am quite prepared to answer any questions.

Chairman: Had you monetary transactions with Sir Arthur Vicars?

Shackleton: I had, sir. Sir Arthur Vicars guaranteed two bills for me.

Chairman: What were those bills – you need not tell us unless you like – what were the dates of those bills, and what were the sums?

Shackleton: The sums were – one was for £650. None of this will appear in the press?

Chairman: I must warn you before you go any further that what you are saying now is being taken down by the shorthand writer; it will be printed, and it may be published.

Shackleton: Then I consider that I should have been told of this beforehand. I do not mean it disrespectfully, but I think it is rather unfair that I should have been allowed to make these statements, because it is a serious matter in business. I was given to understand that the investigation was private. It has been stated in the papers that it is private.

Chairman: It is private in this sense, that the public are not present here; but the evidence is being taken down and will be printed and may be published.

Shackleton: Then I think that that statement should have been given to me before. My reason is this, that it would be very injurious to me in business were it known that at a period when I was engaged in a rather large business transaction I was absolutely in monetary difficulties to any extent.

Jones: This statement has been made by other witnesses, and therefore it is already done.

Shackleton: Thank you very much. I have not been told fully. The first intimation I got of this Commission was last Saturday, at San Remo, that it was to take place tomorrow, Friday, and thereupon I wired to know if my evidence was required. I had not received your summons to attend. It was not posted from London till the 10th of January, and did not reach San Remo till Monday, the 13th, and I wired to Sir James Dougherty to know if I should attend. And I wired directly after I got the letter, which was sent on from my London club.

Chairman: I told you the reason I was asking these questions was not from any idle curiosity of our own, but because statements had been already made to us, and I wished you to have a full opportunity of telling us the facts?

Shackleton: Thank you, sir. Then may I continue? I think the matter was £600, and I think £750, the £750 at a later date.

Chairman: What was the date, you say, of the £750?

Shackleton: It would have been some time in 1906, I imagine towards the middle of 1906.

Chairman: Have you any idea of when those bills came due?

Shackleton: One became due at the end of August 1907, and the last instalment of the £650 bill was paid, I think, at the end of August. I am not a bit clear, but I could easily trace it for you.

Chairman: I understand Sir Arthur Vicars was in these bills as your security. Had you any counter security to give him?

Shackleton: Oh, certainly I could give a counter security.

Chairman: Did you? Had he any security?

Shackleton: He had none at the time.

Chairman: Can you tell us now in whose hands those bills were?

Shackleton: With Messrs Wilton and Co., of 199 Piccadilly, Professional moneylenders and bill discounters; and also Wolff and Hollander, in Tottenham Court Road, furniture men.

Chairman: At the same time that you had these monetary transactions with Sir Arthur Vicars had you also transactions with Mr Goldney?

Shackleton: Yes; Mr Goldney guaranteed a £1,500 bill for me to these moneylenders.

Jones: Did Sir Arthur Vicars have any of the money of those two bills?

Shackleton: £100 in the last bill of 1907. The bill was not so big. It was a renewed bill with an increase of £100. The £650 bill was renewed, I think, in July last, about the 15th of last July, for £750; £100 of it was for Sir Arthur Vicars.

Chairman: Was that the consideration for his backing the bill for you?

Shackleton: I do not know what it was. I do not know what was in his mind.

Starkie: Who proposed that the renewal should be for £750?

Shackleton: I did. Sir Arthur Vicars wanted me to borrow money for him at the time, and I did not want to do so. I could have paid the bill there and then, but it would have meant my selling stocks and shares I held at a very big sacrifice at the moment, and I preferred not to do so, partly because the selling of these stocks would be known to several people whom I did not wish to know that I was in difficulties. I may mention at the outset, in defence of myself, that the first bill – for £1,200 – which Goldney backed I never had a penny of. It was to save a friend of mine from being made bankrupt.

Chairman: When was that?

Shackleton: The matter extended for two years, and it was renewed again. It would run into January 1906. I do not want to give the gentleman's name, because he is now in a very important position, but I can prove it if necessary, and he will come forward if necessary, and his solicitor will. I do not know his official residence now.

Chairman: Was that £1,200, the original sum, carried on?

Shackleton: It was carried on, and mounted to £1,500.

Chairman: What was the date of the £1,500 bill?

Shackleton: I think it must have been May or so of 1906. It was not due, I think, till the end of 1907.

Chairman: That was also payable by instalments?

Shackleton: By instalments, all of which I kept paying up.

Chairman: Can you give us any idea, did you get the full amount of these bills?

Shackleton: No, sir, I did not. I was paying heavy interest. I was paying 10 per cent, and I paid so much additional. It worked out, I should say, 50 per cent. They charge for certain things; they put it in such a way, discount and so much.

Chairman: When were those bills ultimately settled?

Shackleton: I fancy in September 1907. I could get the exact dates. There is a letter which would convey fully to you the date. (Witness handed in the following letter.)


Abbot's Barton Canterbury

*26th August 1907*

My dear F., Frank tells me you are going to fix up everything for him and me on Tuesday or one day this week. This being so I am giving Frank a sum of £250 to give you from me through his solicitor, Sir George Lewis, in payment of the sums you advanced to me for changing house and for additional expenses for our joint house and household, etc.

I note you claim £300, but as there are sundry outstanding accounts due from you on our joint accounts, which Seymour, as you know, kindly promised to go into with me on my return next month, I think it will be quite fair for me to pay you the balance when I can send you a full statement of account, and whatever sum is owing to you I shall send you a cheque for, and if it is the other way on I know you will send me one.

Our accounts are so mixed that I really do not know how they stand between us. Sir George Lewis will hand you the £250 when you hand over to him the two cancelled bills of £600 and £750.

Now that you evidently know the whereabouts of the jewels, from what you have said to both Frank and me, I hope that you have told Mr Kane everything calculated to facilitate matters.

Please write here, as I am staying on here for a little rest. Who have you been staying with at Bembridge? You rush about so, it is difficult to know your address. My brother Harry has gone to Brighton for a day or two, but will be back in London this week in case you want to see him.

Yours in haste, A . Vicars, Ulr.

Chairman: I see he was staying with Mr Goldney at this time, at his friend's house. And 'Frank', I suppose, is Mr Goldney?

Shackleton: Mr Bennett Goldney.

Chairman: Now, you have handed in this letter from Sir Arthur Vicars. I must call your attention to this part of the letter – 'Now, that you evidently know the whereabouts of the jewels, from what you have said to both Frank and me, I hope that you have told Mr Kane everything calculated to facilitate matters.' What does that refer to?

Shackleton: It refers to a letter from me to Sir Arthur Vicars reproaching him for not having told me the jewels were found. I was staying at Harrogate, I think, on that date, and a visitor came up to me and said, holding a paper in his hand: 'Mr Shackleton, the jewels have been found' or 'they say the jewels have been found'. And I wrote to Sir Arthur Vicars reproaching him for not having told me that they were found. I wrote to Mr Pierce Mahony, the Cork Herald, in the same strain and he wrote back to say that it was only a newspaper rumour. That is exactly what happened.

Chairman: And upon that he said: 'You evidently know the whereabouts of the jewels?'

Shackleton: Yes, because Mr Goldney went to Scotland Yard after I had seen him and told them there that I knew where they were. I had met Mr Goldney at the Club and I said: 'Why didn't you tell me the jewels were recovered?' He said, 'Are they?' and I said, 'Yes'. And he said: 'I never heard of it. Are you sure?' I said, 'Yes. I had it on good authority'. I think it was Sir Patrick Coll, who was Law Officer of the Crown at one period. He was staying at the Crown Hotel in Harrogate, and he called my attention to it and the matter was discussed. His son, who was also there, told me later that I was suspected of having taken the jewels, which, unfortunately, I have been by Sir Arthur Vicars and by Mr Goldney. They have left no stone unturned to suggest such.

Chairman: Then he says: 'I hope you have told Mr Kane everything.' Had you an interview with Inspector Kane?

Shackleton: I had many interviews with Mr Kane, and I told him absolutely everything I could possibly think of to facilitate matters from the first day that I left here. I came over here on Monday 8th July. I had seen Mr Kane at Scotland Yard on the afternoon of the 8th, having read in the paper for the first time of the loss of the jewels.

Chairman: He was in the office here then?

Shackleton: On the 8th of July he was in London, at Scotland Yard. I saw him in Scotland Yard and brought to him a copy of the Statutes of the Order of St Patrick, thinking that they might be able to make blocks of the drawings.

I had wired to Sir Arthur Vicars about the loss of the jewels and he wired back and asked me to bring to Scotland Yard copies of the Statutes of the Order of St Patrick, which I did. I crossed that night to Dublin and was in Dublin on Tuesday morning at 7 St James's Terrace. I went back, I believe, the same week, or in about a week's time.

Chairman: Can you tell us when you had last been in Dublin?

Shackleton: Yes, the 7th of June, I think.

Chairman: Did you leave Dublin on the 7th of June?

Shackleton: Yes, I think so. I could find out for a certainty because I was at St Anne's, Clontarf, whatever was the date of that Garden Party, I was there.

(To Sir John Ross) You were there, Sir John Ross, at St Anne's, Clontarf, at the Garden Party that day?

Chairman: Were you ever back again in Dublin till July?

Shackleton: No, not till the morning of the 9th.

(To Sir John Ross) Can you recollect the date of Lady Ardilaun's Garden Party, Sir John?

Sir John Ross: No, I do not remember.

Shackleton: I know I crossed that night in the same boat with Lady Ardilaun. She was going to her sister, who was dying, it was on the 6th or 7th of June. I left Dublin on the 6th or 7th of June. I returned to Dublin afterwards, crossing from London on the night of the 8th of July.

Chairman: If it were suggested here that after you left early in June you might have come here to Dublin and stayed at the North Wall and not gone to Sir Arthur Vicars at all that time, would it be true?

Shackleton: It would not be true, sir. Can you give me a hint – a few days, or a week, or for what period you absolutely want my movements?

Chairman: I think the suggestion that was thrown out was that you might have come back to Dublin between the 7th of June, or whatever the time was, when you left on that occasion, and the date of your coming back in July – that you might have come back to Dublin and stayed at the North Wall?

Shackleton: Well, sir, I never did. But I think I could trace all my movements, because the London clubs are in the habit of noting whenever a member is in the house; it is down in the day-book, and I could trace it from that; but I have reason to believe that that has already been done by Scotland Yard and verified, I know, from the 4th of July. May I have that letter from Sir Arthur Vicars?

Chairman: Now, about the money matters. Sir George Lewis had this money in his hands; was this paid in August 1907?

Shackleton: Yes, it was paid; that is, my money.

Chairman: But you were to hand him back two cancelled bills for £600 and £750?

Shackleton: Yes.

Chairman: Now, who paid that money?

Shackleton: I paid that money. It was my own money absolutely. I don't know the exact date, but I sold a good many shares I had. I cannot trace exactly the date. It was my own money, certainly.

Chairman: If Sir Arthur Vicars had got part of the money out of these bills, why did you pay the whole?

Shackleton: Well, the state of the matter was that I borrowed money for Sir Arthur Vicars with the idea of helping him, and in addition to the sum he had before. I didn't want to come down on him any more than I could help. They said I must pay the bills up and I said I must sell more shares at a loss, and I must ask you to pay me back the £300 you owe me.

Chairman: Did that include the £100 that he had got out of the bill?

Shackleton: That included the £100; the other £200 were totally different matters.

Chairman: It was stated here that considerable pressure had been brought to bear upon you by Sir George Lewis?

Shackleton: Absolutely none. I had extreme difficulty in getting my money from Sir George Lewis.

Chairman: I see Sir Arthur Vicars says: 'Sir George Lewis will hand you the £250 when you hand over to him the two cancelled bills of £600 and £750?'

Shackleton: I did. I handed these over then but I didn't get the money. They wanted me to sign that I had no claim on Sir Arthur Vicars. Does that letter say that he is retaining any money for household accounts?

Chairman: (Re-reads letter) You say that you did hand over the bills?

Shackleton: I did, and I had to wait at least a week. I had several letters on the subject, and they asked me to sign a full discharge of any liability for further claims on Sir Arthur Vicars, which I refused to do.

Chairman: Now, assuming that you are going to put in these other letters, which I think it would be well to reserve till the end of the evidence, do you tell me this, that you came over on the evening of the 8th, or the morning of the 9th July?

Shackleton: I crossed on the evening of the 8th, and arrived in the morning and went to St James's Terrace.

Chairman: Whom did you find there?

Shackleton: Mr Bennett Goldney and Sir Arthur Vicars. Sir Arthur Vicars was in bed. Mr Goldney and I had breakfast together and came straight on here to be here at half past nine to meet the authorities who were coming to investigate the loss.

Chairman: Had you any conversation with Sir Arthur Vicars and Mr Goldney that morning?

Shackleton: I must have had, because we were in the habit of walking into one another's rooms and talking while we dressed.

Chairman: There was a considerable amount of conversation about the loss of the jewels?

Shackleton: Naturally so, sir.

Chairman: Did you tell them that you had crossed over in the boat with a lady with whom you had some conversation about the jewels?

Shackleton: Yes; the Marchioness of Ormonde.

Chairman: Did you tell them that the lady, whoever she was, said how strange a thing it was that you were telling her at lunch the other day that you would not be surprised to wake any morning and find the Crown Jewels were stolen?

Shackleton: What she said to me was – my sleeping carriage was next hers: 'Oh, Mr Shackleton, how extraordinary; poor Sir Arthur Vicars, I am sorry for him; isn't it an odd thing – Constance and I were just talking – we were just saying how odd it was, that remark of yours, at lunch the other day.' My remark was, I think, on the 4th of July, at lunch at Lady Ormonde's in Upper Brook Street, and the conversation turned on Sir Arthur Vicars, and some remark was made about Sir Arthur Vicars — some passing remark I think about his being fussy, or something like that, was said by somebody present — and I said, 'But he has a great deal of responsibility, and he is very proud of his office'. Some remark like that, which Lady Ormonde backed me up in, and then it got into talk of the jewels, and I said: 'Oh, I should never be surprised to hear that they were stolen some day.' I never considered they were safe. Afterwards Rear-Admiral Tudor told me that he made the same remark to Lady Mayo, that he didn't think they were safe. I met him in Shropshire in September and in talking to him I told him that I made the remark, which was very unfortunate for me, because it was taken up by many people. I told the story against myself, and in actual innocence of the thing; I said it in the most innocent way, and the very remark of itself proves that, but it has been talked about, and I happened to mention it to Rear-Admiral Tudor and he made the remark, 'I said that very thing to Lady Mayo'.

Chairman: Why did you think the jewels were unsafe?

Shackleton: Well, for many reasons. I considered there were too many keys of the outer door. Another thing that I considered was so dangerous was the fact that there is a skylight upstairs, and nearly the whole Castle communicates by the roofs with their skylights, which I have frequently seen open in the summer time.

I considered nothing could be easier also than for a person to enter the premises in broad daylight when the office messenger might be for some time upstairs with Sir Arthur Vicars, and hide himself in the cellars all day long and come out again at night and take whatever he wanted and the next day walk out calmly past the sentry, because people were in the habit of walking in through this door without ringing the bell.

I have often walked in here and the office messenger was up with Sir Arthur Vicars, and I have walked in and taken the key out of the grill. I have often done it, pretending that I had something to do, when I saw people that I didn't know in the office.

Chairman: You formed the idea that the jewels were unsafe from the condition of the office?

Shackleton: Not the jewels particularly, but the whole place. I spoke of the jewels on that occasion; I mentioned them specially because they were the subject under discussion. People walked in here when the grill was wide open, and I have gone to the office messenger and told him to shut the door in case he had to go up. There have been people heaps of times in and out this office, and I was never satisfied with anything.

Chairman: How did it occur to you that anybody could get access to the safe in which the jewels were?

Shackleton: Only by using a duplicate key. The use of a dummy key never occurred to me for a moment. My idea was that the burglar could secrete himself and by the light outside he could have sufficient light to work in here with any instrument to open the safe. That was my idea. It was only in a very general way. I am now bringing it down to a narrow point. The idea of a duplicate key, or the identical key, never entered my head. But the condition in which the lock appeared when I saw it taken to pieces on the morning of the 9th July 1907 showed me that it must have been the most perfect duplicate of the original key.

Chairman: Had you yourself access at any time to the keys in Sir Arthur Vicars' house?

Shackleton: I might have access to this extent, but I have never had occasion to use them. Certainly I could have gone into his room when he was in the bath and taken these keys. I think he did not take them into the bathroom, and when I have gone in to speak to him, when he was in bed, they were under his pillow, and I could have, very easily, had I so wished, gone to his room and taken an impression of the key or taken the original key off if I had known it, and walked away with that key and replaced it quite easily if necessary, because I was in and out, talking. I don't say that I was always going into his room, because he used to grumble that I got up so early. He said that I was like a Donegal peasant getting up at cockcrow; but I used to go to bed early, which was one of his grievances because he had no companion.

Chairman: Could you have taken possession of the keys and made wax impressions of them, or other impressions during the time he was in his bath?

Shackleton: If I knew how to do so, quite easily. I could have taken it and kept it for a week and put a key almost like it on the chain trusting to his never having occasion to go to the safe for another week or so. Anyone could have done that. When I say myself, you asked me if I could and I said I could, being in the house. That refers to any inmate of the house. I don't want to pile up a case against myself, but it would be quite easy for me to do so.

Chairman: It was stated here this morning that Sir Arthur Vicars made a statement that on a day, I think it was the King's birth-day, the 28th June, Sir Arthur Vicars came down to the office and the office was closed, as it was a holiday, and that he had been looking for his latchkey in his own house for the purpose of coming down here to open the door, and that the latchkey could not be found? This was in 1907.

Shackleton: I was not in Ireland on the 28th June.

Chairman: He said he could not find the key of his office in his own house, and he had to get a key from the detective to open the door, and he never found that latchkey till July, when you returned. And when you returned to Dublin he found the key left on his dressing-table, just where it had been when it was taken. Did you take that latchkey?

Shackleton: I did not, sir, at any time. This is the first I have heard of it.

Chairman: There is no truth in the suggestion – because that undoubtedly is the suggestion – that you took possession of this key on or before the 28th of June and did not return it till you came back on the 9th July?

Shackleton: Absolutely untrue, and this is the first I heard of it. I am quite willing to give any evidence I possibly can. I understood this Commission was not to find the thief, but was to find whether Sir Arthur Vicars had exercised proper care of the jewels.

Chairman: Yes, but Sir Arthur Vicars' custody of the keys is a very important element in that?

Shackleton: All right, sir. But still it is only right for myself that I should have a chance of having it stated. I am perfectly willing to swear that I never took it.

Chairman: How did you know that the safe key was kept under Sir Arthur Vicars' pillow?

Shackleton: Because I often saw the bunch of keys half lying out, and I assume that the key was on that chain because he stated it. I always understood it was on it because he was so anxious about this bunch of keys.

Chairman: Did you know that there was a second key for the safe?

Shackleton: No, never; not till after the loss of the jewels, when I heard that there was a second key hidden somewhere in the house, which Sir Arthur Vicars had hidden so well that he could not find it himself.

Starkie: Did you know where Sir Arthur Vicars kept the key of the strong-room?

Shackleton: I do not know where he kept it; I do not know where it was kept; I am not sure he had a key of the strong-room; I thought the office messenger had it.

Chairman: I think, Mr Solicitor, that I have asked all that we require. Perhaps you may have some questions to ask him.

Solicitor-general: Kindly tell me, Mr Shackleton, when first you heard of the holding of the present Commission?

Shackleton: Saturday night; well, I had a cutting sent to me that there was going to be a Commission tomorrow, that is, Friday. The paper stated that it would be on Friday week, a paper of about Thursday last; that was the first I heard of it. Then I saw a further account of it next day, that it was on Friday. I wired on Saturday to know would my evidence be required.

Solicitor-general: Were you at San Remo?

Shackleton: Yes, and on the Monday following I was at Nice for the day, and when I came in I received this envelope, which was posted on Friday and arrived at San Remo on 12th, and delivered at the hotel during the daytime on Monday; but I had gone by an early train to Nice, and I had finished reading this when I got a telegram in answer to mine, from Sir James Dougherty. This notice had been handed in at my club in London.

Solicitor-general: Then, as I understand, you have come direct from San Remo here?

Shackleton: Yes; I started at four o'clock on Tuesday morning. I arrived in Paris at half past five and left by the nine o'clock boat for London, arriving in London at half past five, and took the

Irish Mail and arrived here this morning.

Solicitor-general: Now, you told the Commissioners what your arrangements were as regards the house in St James's Terrace, Clonskeagh. Have you continued that arrangement as regards the payment of the wages of servants, or when was that discontinued?

Shackleton: It was discontinued at the request of Sir Arthur Vicars and his family. It was really first written to me by Major Vicars asking me as writs had been served at the house. It was some time in August, the final break-up; it was to release me of my payment of half the rent.

Solicitor-general: Were writs served at the house against you?

Shackleton: They were against me. I do not know the exact position at the present moment. I am still paying my share of the rent, because the owner of the house wrote to me to state that she could not get money from Sir Arthur Vicars, and therefore I must still hold to my original lease. I paid my share of the last three quarters. My half was due some time ago.

Solicitor-general: You have told us that to the best of your recollection you left Ireland on the 7th June 1907 – the afternoon of Lady Ardilaun's garden party?

Shackleton: Yes; that is the only way I can fix it, because she crossed over the same night.

Solicitor-general: And were you in London continuously from the 7th or 8th of June till you came to Dublin here on the morning of the 8th July?

Shackleton: I was also at Penshurst, in Kent. I was certainly there for the weekend of the 6th to the 8th of July, because I was coming up in the train with the owner of the house, my friend Lord Ronald Sutherland Gower, who first saw it in the paper and called my attention to it. I think on one weekend before that the Duke of Argyll was there also. I remember coming up certainly with the Duke of Argyll one Monday in July.

Solicitor-general: But except for those two weekend visits were you continuously in London from your arrival there on the 8th of June?

Shackleton: Yes, unless I went down to my house in Devonshire. I do not think I was down there.

Solicitor-general: During that time did you visit your club day by day?

Shackleton: If I was in London I would do so, at least one of my clubs; I have four clubs in London.

Solicitor-general: And did the Scotland Yard officials examine the entries?

Shackleton: I think so, because they were very particular in making their investigations to know my whereabouts for the period when I left in June till I came back in July.

Solicitor-general: Do I understand you to state that on the 4th of July you lunched with Lady Ormonde at Brook Street?

Shackleton: The 4th or 5th of July. I could fix it by writing to her. I could wire to her now; she is at Kilkenny, I think.

Solicitor-general: And could you tell us, did you immediately, or some time after the robbery, get a telegram at all from Sir Arthur Vicars asking you to come over; do you recollect?

Shackleton: I only got a telegram in answer to mine, asking was it true about the jewels. He wired me: 'Yes, and my mother's also, and if you have a copy of the Statutes of the Order take them to Scotland Yard to have blocks made of those plates.' I was to come over in any case. I wired from Penshurst to Canterbury, to Mr Goldney, to know when he was crossing, so as to cross with him, and I got back a wire to say he had already crossed on Sunday.

Solicitor-general: You, as I understand, had got a telegram from Sir Arthur Vicars asking you to come over after the robbery was discovered?

Shackleton: He may have wired, too, about arranging. He knew I was coming over. The arrangement had been made a week previously, but he may have said, 'Come over with Frank' and I may have had a telegram in reference to that, but it was only a matter in confirmation of an existing arrangement.

Solicitor-general: When did you, as a matter of fact, arrive in Dublin after the jewel robbery had been discovered?

Shackleton: I arrived on the morning of Tuesday the 8th.

Solicitor-general: And then, as you told us, you went to Sir Arthur Vicars' house at Clonskeagh. Did you, on that morning, discuss with Sir Arthur Vicars as to how, possibly, the robbery could have occurred?

Shackleton: I am not quite sure that I did. Not to any extent that I can remember. No, I did not. When I saw him he was in a sort of condition that he really did not know what to think. He seemed quite overwhelmed by the whole thing.

Solicitor-general: And did you and he discuss it on various occasions during the week?

Shackleton: Oh, yes, of course we discussed it, very much so, because a person came from the Irish Exhibition to say she could tell us something about the loss of the jewels, and I promptly went off at once to the Italian section of the Exhibition and found a woman who told us that her daughter had a vision, and Sir Arthur Vicars arranged a séance of clairvoyants to see where the key was on the following Sunday at St James's Terrace.

Solicitor-general: Now, how long was Mr Goldney over here while you were here?

Shackleton: I do not imagine that he was here more than a few days. He arrived on Sunday and left probably Wednesday or Thursday.

Solicitor-general: Did you and he and Sir Arthur ever discuss together how possibly the robbery could have occurred?

Shackleton: Oh yes we did, and talked about it generally, and must have done so. It was most natural. I am sure we talked fully about it.

Solicitor-general: Can you tell the Commissioners at all whether there was any speculation on the part of either Mr Goldney, Sir Arthur Vicars or yourself as to how it occurred?

Shackleton: Oh, there was nothing remarkable at all. We came to the conclusion that somebody at some period must have got hold of a key and made an impression.

Solicitor-general: When you were here did you ascertain at all from anyone that the strong-room door had been found open on the morning of Saturday 6th July?

Shackleton: I was told that by the office messenger when I came over here. He told me that he told Sir Arthur Vicars on the morning of the day on which the jewels were first missed that when he came in the strong-room door had been found open by the office cleaner and that she had removed the keys that were always hanging in the grille and had put them into an envelope and left them addressed to the office messenger on his table, where he found them on entering the office. This was reported to Sir Arthur Vicars, and apparently Sir Arthur Vicars did not investigate the strong-room to see if anything had been touched.

Chairman: Sir Arthur Vicars had not spoken to you about the strong-room having been found open?

Shackleton: No; I learned it here. It was only from the office messenger I heard it. When Sir Arthur Vicars did refer to it afterwards I remarked to him about the strong-room. I said: 'Why did not you examine the strong-room?' He said: 'Oh, I was so worried that I did not think. The police are making great capital out of this, my not having told them in proper time, and unfortunately the police have been annoyed at its not having been conveyed to them at once.' He seemed rather vexed with me, because it seemed a natural thing, when he was told of the strong-room being open, where there were collars and maces and things, that he would examine it.

I did not know about it in the morning till I came in here. It was in here I learned it, not from Sir Arthur Vicars. I think I am quite clear on that. It made an impression on me at the time. And I think it was remarkable, quite remarkable, that he never trusted me with the key of the safe and yet sent down this messenger with it. He had a sort of mania. He used to go round at night feeling that every one of these presses were shut. Many a time ten minutes passed after my getting a cab for him in waiting while he ran round to see that everything was shut.

Chairman: Did you ever put it to him that while it might be one thing to fabricate a key for the safe it was also possible to fabricate a key of the strong-room – was that matter discussed?

Shackleton: Oh, yes we discussed it, that they must have fabricated two keys and that it must have taken a couple of years' time. And I also asked why should nothing be touched in the strong-room, because there was no sign of anything having been disturbed at any period. Why should everything be left as it should be in the strong-room?

And I said to him; 'When you found the strong-room was open and examined it', for I had not known that he had not examined it at that time, 'and found everything correct, surely it would have struck you about the safe?'

He said: 'I don't remember. Stivey might have said it to me when I was running up the stairs.' I did not press the matter very much, because he did not seem pleased that he had been blamed by the police or that he did not mention the thing sooner.

Solicitor-general: You told us before of a conversation at breakfast on the morning of your arrival?

Shackleton: I think it was up in the bedroom. I think Mr Goldney was shaving, and I had just had my bath, and we were talking of things in general, and I said I just came across with Lady Ormonde, and she said was not it funny that I should have made the remark to her? And she remembered it. I forgot it myself till she brought it to my recollection.

Solicitor-general: And you found Rear-Admiral Tudor made the same remark?

Shackleton: To Lady Mayo, I think, some months afterwards. He put his hand on me (gestured) and he said: 'Where are the jewels?' 'It is not a joking matter at all', I said, because a telegram supposed to have been in my handwriting was sent to the Lord Lieutenant. And I told him it was rather a serious thing for me, there being so much talk of my being connected so much with the loss, and he said: 'I would not have said it if so.' And then I told him the various things that had been said against me, including the remark I made to Lady Ormonde, and he said; 'I made the same remark to Lady Mayo, and objected to the custody of the plate here.' And he said he did not think the things were safe. I did not know where it was to be put, but he spoke about it in general terms, and said he had discussed it with Lady Mayo at the meeting of the Committee of the

Hibernia presentation.

Chairman: It was some months afterwards that Rear-Admiral Tudor told this gentleman, but Admiral Tudor's remark was made before the discovery?

Shackleton: Yes. I said to him that it seemed rather absurd that it should be used against me, and he said, 'Well, I made the same remark', and it was just as much as to say, 'Well, it might have been used against me'.

Solicitor-general: I am unwilling to go into the details of the question of your pecuniary relations with Sir Arthur Vicars and Goldney. Do I understand you to say distinctly that it was your money paid off these bills?

Shackleton: My money, sir, my own money. It was with my money that I paid it. I do not say that I may not have borrowed it, that it was not given to me, or anything like that, but it was absolutely my own money. I do not deny that people might have helped me, and I do not say that it was the case or that it was not the case, but I say that at the time I paid that money it was my own money, for that purpose.

Solicitor-general: Now, you have told the Commission that there was a number of letters which you had in your possession dealing with the matter? Are you willing to exhibit those to the Commissioners?

Shackleton: Well, sir, I will tell you exactly my position. As far as I can see certain statements were made about me and my finances, and it certainly appeared to me that they did not look favourable to me, but at the same time I would really much sooner not show these letters, because in a way they are letters that are very private, referring to his own affairs, and it seems hardly fair to Sir Arthur Vicars that I should show them. That is the exact position.

Chairman: I think it is not necessary to insist upon this. We have had already the fact that there were money transactions between them. I will let the letters go.

Shackleton: But I have come a long way to try and do my best. The point is this, that I should not be criticized as having done anything unmanly in laying these letters before you. I give you these letters because I have heard so much recently from private friends who have written to me telling me about things said about me, and I suppose the time has come when I should –

Chairman: I think it is only fair that we should look at these letters, and if we think they are relevant to the inquiry we will use them, and if not we will return them to you?

Shackleton: The position is this: that I lent Sir Arthur Vicars money in small sums, and writs were served, and I had money, but I should have had to withdraw from a financial undertaking, which it took 18 months to complete, and I should have had to expose to the financial world in which I was working that I was in financial difficulties, and I kept a flat in London and a house in Devonshire, and without disclosing that difficulty I succeeded in carrying out a negotiation in which I was engaged which the least breath of suspicion that I was in difficulties would have ruined.

Chairman: We will not use these letters at present, but would you keep these letters. You will not destroy these letters? (Letters handed back to witness.)

Shackleton: Do you say it is essential that I should keep them? But I do not think I was actually fairly treated in the matter, as I have been rather misrepresented to my friends, and more or less to the public in general, as regards the way in which I have treated Sir Arthur Vicars.

Chairman: I am speaking for your own interest and for your own protection. I think you ought to keep these letters. We do not wish to use them.

Shackleton: I think it is only right. I have my family to consider as well as myself.

Chairman: We keep this letter of the 25th of August, in which he says, 'now that you evidently know the whereabouts of the jewels'. We have looked at those letters, Mr Solicitor, and though they are important in some respects, we do not think that they are strictly relevant to our inquiry.

Shackleton: They entirely refer to financial matters between myself and Sir Arthur Vicars.

Solicitor-general: Were they prior to the discovery of the robbery?

Shackleton: Up to the time of the robbery. There is one I should like to use publicly if necessary in the statement I have made. It is in reference to getting a loan of £100, because it was denied. That is a letter of the 22nd April 1907. (Hands letter to Solicitor-General.)

Solicitor-general: (Reads from letter dated 22nd April 1907, from Sir Arthur Vicars, 7 St James's Terrace, to witness, mentioning household financial difficulties as to rent, food, and gas.) 'So I should be grateful to you if you would manage to get a loan for me, as I suggested in my last.'

Shackleton: The rest does not refer to any matter of importance, but only that point, that there is certainly an instance in which he wished me to borrow money.

Solicitor-general: Was it at all explained to you by Mr Bennett Goldney or by Sir Arthur Vicars why in September 1907 you were asked to pay up those bills?

Shackleton: The reason was because in the face of the publicity that the question got, it might tell against Sir Arthur Vicars and Mr Goldney with people who would not know the reason the money was borrowed, and that they might not have any of the proceeds. Mr Goldney never had any of the proceeds, nor had a share of that bill; but it might have told against Goldney, and he was anxious that it should be paid off at once. Then as to Sir Arthur Vicars, he had had £100 on one of those bills, and the reason he wanted it to be paid off was that he said it was serious with a cloud hanging over the office to have any financial transactions between us.

Solicitor-general: And with a view to that it was communicated to you that the money should be paid off?

Shackleton: Yes; and also, one of his brothers did not like to have this liability hanging over Sir Arthur Vicars. One of his brothers or the two of his brothers, the family, objected to the liability hanging over Sir Arthur Vicars, and wanted me to assign the furniture and plate lying at St James's Terrace if I did not pay it off. But I did pay it off.

Solicitor-general: It is only fair to you that I should ask you definitely was the payment off of these bills at that time when they pressed you to pay them in any sense at all in relation to the jewel robbery? Had the request that you should pay off the bill at that time in September any relation at all to the jewel robbery? Was there any imputation against you by them at that time that you were concerned in the robbery?

Shackleton: No, not at that time. The imputations were not till afterwards.

Solicitor-general: And do I understand that the ground of the request to pay off was that, having regard to all that had occurred, it would be unfortunate if financial relations turned out to be subsisting between you and them?

Shackleton: Yes; I have a letter which absolutely conveyed that to me, and first it was written by one of Sir Arthur Vicars' brothers to me. The brother wrote to me that it was serious for Sir Arthur Vicars at this moment, and also serious for me. I can send that letter to you.

Solicitor-general: It is only fair to ask you: at that time, was there any imputation against you by either Mr Goldney or Sir Arthur Vicars? At the time when you were paying off those bills?

Shackleton: The first I ever heard against me was that the detectives had a telegram which was sent to the Lord Lieutenant saying, 'Jewels are in box, 9 Hadley Street, Dublin'. I had just come up to London from Southsea. I had been at Fort Blockhouse, and I came up to town and saw Inspector Kane. He came to the club, and he said: 'Oh, I thought you were not coming up till Wednesday.' And I said: 'I came up today.' He said: 'I want to show you something at Scotland Yard.' I went to Scotland Yard, and he said: 'Whose writing is that?' He held up what appeared to be an ordinary telegram form such as are to be found in all telegraph offices, but all folded up except just a portion of the writing which was the word 'Dublin'. I said: 'That is mine.' I would have sworn, if I had not seen the rest of it, that it was my writing. And then the telegram was opened out, and I saw that it was not written by me.

Solicitor-general: What was that telegram?

Shackleton: It was a telegram sent to the Lord Lieutenant from Great Malvern. It said: 'Jewels are in box, 9 Hadley Street, Dublin.' Sir Arthur Vicars was at Canterbury at the time, and he was telegraphed for by Scotland Yard to come to see if he could identify the handwriting as mine. He was shown the one word and asked in my presence who wrote it, and he said, quite like that: 'I suppose you did.' He did not answer Inspector Kane, and he said 'you' and 'I suppose', and they all looked at one another. Major Vicars was there at the time too. And then the thing was opened out, and he still contended it was mine, and I said: You might believe it was mine.'

Chairman: When the telegram was opened out?

Shackleton: We all went to Scotland Yard, and the telegram was opened out at Scotland Yard and carefully read over. I said to him: 'Well, you do not believe it is mine, do you?' He said: 'Yes I do.' And I said: 'You may think the writing is like mine, but you do not think I wrote it, do you?' 'Well', he said, 'I do think you wrote it. You have not assisted the police?' He generally conveyed to me that he more or less suspected me.

Inspector Kane said: 'Now, Mr Shackleton, you will not be astonished at whatever position', or words to that effect, 'the police assume', or 'what notice they will take of this statement', or 'what action'. In other words, it conveyed to me that I might be arrested on suspicion.

First of all, I think it is criminal to send a telegram or anything of that nature to the King or his representative. At any rate, I did not know what might happen. I went to my flat that night and expected to be arrested next day, and I sent a district messenger to my brother in Devonshire to come up, and I stayed in London, and I kept Scotland Yard posted of my movements of the day in case they wanted to arrest me. And that was the first time there was anything against me. The telegram had been sent on the 28th of August, and this was in September.

Solicitor-general: Was it your writing?

Shackleton: No. I was never informed, or relieved of the suspense and unpleasantness I felt with regard to that telegram; but I have been informed since, but not till quite a long time afterwards, that Scotland Yard had completely investigated the matter and found that the telegram was sent by a gentleman of high repute in Great Malvern whose wife had a vision, or thought she had a vision, and saw the words '9 Hadley Street,

Dublin'. Nor have I been informed for one moment by Sir Arthur Vicars that it was so, and the greatest capital was made out of it, and it was told against me everywhere.

Solicitor-general: I think it is only just to this gentleman to state that the matter has been investigated as regards this telegram by the police officials and authorities, and it has been discovered that the telegram was sent by a gentleman of high repute in circumstances of the character he has just indicated. That is the information in the possession of the police relating to that telegram, and also to a subsequent one which was sent also to Lord Aberdeen from the same post office on the 4th of September. That telegram was sent by A. Bullock Webster, and whatever bearing the incident might have on the case, it is only right, in justice to the witness, that that should be mentioned to the Commission. I thought it was only just to the witness that the matter should be stated to the Commission. Of course that is only one aspect of the whole case.

(To witness) You say that suspicion has been thrown on you. I must ask you a definite question, and you will understand that you need not answer it if you do not like. Did you, or did you not, take the jewels?

Shackleton: I did not take them; I know nothing of their disappearance; I have no suspicion of anybody.

Solicitor-general: Were you concerned, directly or indirectly, in their taking?

Shackleton: No. I know that I am suspected because I travelled from Paris to Italy about the end of the year. I had gone out there on business. Even a man in the train who didn't know me happened to touch on the jewels, and from what he said I had a feeling that I was suspected. He made a reference to me, and I think I pointed to a printed label hanging on my luggage which was almost as if I had said, 'I am the person'.

I also saw that a paper stated that the jewels had been traced to Paris, and that a Scotland Yard detective visited an important West End club and there saw a member who immediately left for the Continent 'where he now is', and everything fitted into it. Twice I went to Paris, but it was solely connected with financing a business which I helped to bring out at the end of the year, and had it been known that I had ever been in financial straits I would not have been able to bring the thing through.

Solicitor-general: Did anyone in confederacy with you take the jewels?

Shackleton: No. I had no hand in it, nor do I know anybody that took them, nor have I the least suspicion.

Solicitor-general: Or have you any idea as to where they are?

Shackleton: No, not the least idea as to where they are.

Solicitor-general: It would be a desirable matter to get any information that would throw light on the affair of these jewels. Can you assist the Commission in any way in that?

Shackleton: Not in any way, sir; I have absolutely no knowledge of it. I cannot even suggest a possible solution of it other than the one which I have already suggested, namely, that somebody resident in our house at some period, or actually in that house, had access to the key and put on another key.

Solicitor-general: Have you heard any speculation from anyone as to where the jewels possibly may be?

Shackleton: No, sir; other than I was told they were back in the office. I know perfectly well that I am accused of even aiding Lord Haddon in taking them away.

Solicitor-general: You need not mention that?

Shackleton: I am only mentioning what has been said. I would tell you if I knew. I have come all the way from San Remo, and I am not at all strong in health. I have done it at very great sacrifice to myself, and it is hardly likely that I would be here if not to assist. I have come to assist. I am ready to give all the assistance I possibly can, and I consider I answered questions which had no bearing whatever on the question, and I think that ought to convey to you my willingness to give any evidence I can.

Solicitor-general: It was at Harrogate, you say, that you met Sir Patrick Coll?

Shackleton: Yes; in the same hotel.

Solicitor-general: Had you the jewels in your possession, or any knowledge of them, when you were at Harrogate?

Shackleton: No, I never had; I knew nothing about them.

Solicitor-general: Do you know whether Sir Arthur Vicars ever kept a diary?

Shackleton: Yes; he kept an office diary. He certainly had, I know, a private diary. He could tell the dates of everything. Everything was entered up; everybody that came and went. He could tell from his private diary that 'F' arrived at such a time, or 'F' left at such a time. I have occasionally entered letters in his own diary myself.

Solicitor-general: And that diary would show that you were in the house?

Shackleton: Would show that I was in the house, and when I left. One of his letters here refers to keeping a diary.

Solicitor-general: Supposing you left Ireland on the 7th June last year, in the ordinary course would that be in the diary?

Shackleton: That entry would be in the diary.

Solicitor-general: And if you came here to Clonskeagh between that date and the 9th of July and you saw him yourself, would that also appear?

Shackleton: That would be in the diary; he kept a very consistent diary.

Starkie: You have seen the jewels, I suppose?

Shackleton: Oh, yes.

Starkie: When did you last see them?

Shackleton: I think I saw the Lord Lieutenant wearing them at the opening of the Exhibition, but I could not say. I could not say that he wore the jewels.

Starkie: Have you seen them in the safe?

Shackleton: Oh, I have seen Sir Arthur Vicars taking them out and showing them. The last time I saw them, I think, to my recollection, was Horse Show week of 1906, when I think he showed them to Lady Orford and Lady Donegall, who were here at that time.

Starkie: When Sir Arthur Vicars asked you to lend him money or raise money for him, did he offer you any security?

Shackleton: No.

Starkie: Did you ask him for any?

Shackleton: No. Once he gave me back a receipt without a stamp on it.

Chairman: That was the 28th of February?

Shackleton: No, that was the 23rd of July 1904, the money which he offered to pay with 5 per cent interest.

Solicitor-general: Can you tell the Commission when the insignia was worn by His Excellency?

Shackleton: I think on collar days, levees, drawing-rooms and all State functions. There were several collar days, when the Knights wore their collars.

Solicitor-general: Do you remember when His Majesty visited Lord Dudley; did Lord Dudley wear the insignia?

Shackleton: No, I cannot remember. I didn't see Lord Dudley on that occasion; I didn't see him pass at all.

Starkie: Before you left Dublin in June did you hear a rumour that the King was coming in July?

Shackleton: Oh, yes, I think I did; it had been rumoured for some time previously. Oh yes, there was a rumour that Leopards Town Races had been put on for him, or something like that. I know that I was in Ireland when there were races put off to suit his arrival.

Shackleton: Shall I be required again, because I propose going back, and I should be sorry if I should be obliged to do the journey over again. I have just been able to keep up. I suffer very much from internal haemorrhage, and it comes on with the least exertion.

Solicitor-general: I don't think we shall require you again.

Shackleton: One other point. If I am strong enough I shall be going out to Canada during the year. I intended to go last year, but I waited to see my brother off to the South Pole, and so I gave that up

Chairman: We sincerely trust that this investigation will come to an end before you go to Canada.

Solicitor-general: May I read the statement made by the witness to the police? [Reads a statement of the witness in which he referred to his possession of the key of the office door.]

Shackleton: I had forgotten that I had made that statement about the key. The impression must have been naturally in my mind that it was the messenger's key. But I had forgotten that I had already stated here.

Solicitor-general: You say you recollect having the key on a holiday on one occasion about three years ago?

Shackleton: Yes.

Solicitor-general: But have you not told us that you had it on more than one occasion?

Shackleton: I think I must have had it on more than one occasion, but I was absolutely certain of one occasion, and I ought to have said 'at least one occasion'. Now, going over everything, I am sure I had it on more than one occasion. That statement was hurriedly taken down; just to the best of my recollection at the moment.

Solicitor-general: It speaks for itself; but I want to call your attention to the apparent discrepancy, whatever it is worth. In that statement, you say you had the key on one occasion; now you say on more than one occasion?

Shackleton: I should have said 'at least on one occasion'. I must have remembered one occasion. I remember dropping it into the letterbox; that is how I know one occasion.

### Re-examination of Chief Inspector John Kane

Solicitor-general: Mention was made today about the telegram that came from Great Malvern to say 'Jewels in box, 9 Hadley Street, Dublin'. That telegram was unsigned?

Kane: Yes.

Solicitor-general: Have you investigated that matter? And a further telegram sent from the same place by Mr Bullock Webster?

Kane: I have.

Solicitor-general: And have you satisfied yourself that they were sent by Mr Bullock Webster?

Kane: Absolutely.

Solicitor-general: And is he a gentleman of high position?

Kane: Of the highest repute, and he wrote them absolutely bona fide in consequence of a communication made to him by his wife.

Solicitor-general: Were you ever told at any time, by either Mr Goldney or Sir Arthur Vicars, that Mr Shackleton knew the whereabouts of the jewels?

Kane: Oh, yes; by both. They told me that they were fully convinced that Shackleton knew where the jewels were, and that they gathered that from conversations with Shackleton and from some of his letters; but they never could give me any tangible evidence that satisfied me that there was any justification for those suggestions at all.

Chairman: Did they show you any letter on which they founded their suggestions?

Kane: No they did not. It was merely on conversations that came to their knowledge which Mr Shackleton had had with other people.

Starkie: Did you ever trace any fact that would tend to throw suspicion on Mr Shackleton?

Kane: Never.

Starkie: Not a shred of evidence against him?

Kane: Not the remotest. I have repeated to Sir Arthur Vicars and his friends over and over again, and I desire to say that now, when they pestered me with not only suggestions, but direct accusations of Mr Shackleton, that they might as well accuse me, so far as the evidence they produced went to justify them.

Chairman: That is entirely the impression that we have got. And is that the result of your inquiries regarding Mr Shackleton?

Kane: That is the result of my inquiries regarding Mr Shackleton.

Chairman: Did you examine the club books in relation to him in London?

Kane: Oh, yes. I think he has practically accounted for every movement, and he has done everything in his power to supply me with information regarding his movements.

There was an answer which I gave to solicitor-general yesterday in answer to his question as to whether Sir Arthur had ever mentioned the name of any person who had taken impressions of his keys. I said No. I should like to supplement that by the addition of three words, 'except Mr Shackleton'.

\* \* \*

Solicitor-general: It may be well to have it stated on the notes that Miss Gibbon has been called frequently and has not been in attendance.

Secretary: I wrote to her the day before the Commission opened and again yesterday, requesting her attendance, and to my knowledge she has been in the office on several days while the Commission has been sitting, but she has not appeared here.

Solicitor-general: I have the statement she has made to the police, and it might be desirable that the Commission should see it.

Secretary: I have now seen Miss Gibbon in an office upstairs. She declines to appear before the Commission because she is of opinion that the mode of inquiry does not give fair play to her chief, for whom she has every respect and regard. I asked her what she meant by the mode of inquiry, and she said, because it is not a judicial inquiry.

Chairman: Is there anything further?

Solicitor-general: Just one matter. I was asked whether there is in the Statutes any direct prohibition against exhibiting the insignia, and at that time I stated from my recollection that there is not and I think that is borne out by examination of the Statutes, except such prohibition as is implied in the Statute which provides that they are to be deposited in a steel safe in the strong-room of the office. I think a prohibition is necessarily implied in that; but you will have an opportunity of considering the Statutes, of course. There is also one other matter that was mentioned, in connection with the Kildare Street Club. There is in most clubs a book recording the entry and departure of members day by day. I have had inquiries made, and I have ascertained that that practice does not exist in the Kildare Street Club, and that there is no book kept by the hall porter which would tell whether a member was present there on any particular day. There is only one other matter. We intend to call – and this is the last witness – Mr Bond, who is the telephone attendant in the Chief secretary's office. He will give you information as to when it is that he goes away at night.

### Examination of Mr Alexander Loftus Bond

*Bond confirmed that he was the messenger in the Chief Secretary's office and was in attendance on the Under-Secretary and the Assistant Under-Secretary in the Castle. His room was the first to be reached after going upstairs. It adjoined the room of the Under-Secretary, and the Assistant Under-Secretary's room was further along the corridor. He stated that he was in exclusive attendance upon the Exchange telephone, which was situated in his office, except while he was at dinner, between one and two o'clock.*

Solicitor-general: Can you show by the attendance book when it was that you went off duty on the night of the 5th of July?

Bond: I have marked it seven o'clock. (Attendance book produced.)

Solicitor-general: Now, when you leave the office is the Exchange telephone in your room open to any person who chooses to go to it?

Bond: Yes; any person allowed in the Chief Secretary's office could have access to it.

Solicitor-general: The entry door is not locked?

Bond: Not locked.

Solicitor-general: And access to it in no way obstructed?

Bond: No.

Solicitor-general: And you did not return till the following morning?

Bond: Next morning, ten o'clock.

Jones: There would not be many people using that room after you had left, not many as a rule?

Bond: Not many.

Jones: Any person might stay there for a quarter of an hour or so though you were out?

Bond: They could, easily, or perhaps longer.

Solicitor-general: From the corridor, is there a door leading into your room?

Bond: Yes.

Solicitor-general: And what is the second entry?

Bond: When you reach the top of the stairs there is a door that goes to the Under-Secretary's room and the Chief Secretary's room, and there is an ante-room off that, and there is a second door on that side.

Chairman: The doors are always open?

Bond: Always.

Solicitor-general: Who, if anyone, would be in charge of the office after your departure at seven o'clock?

Bond: There is a policeman on duty in the hall, and the reception messenger, when he is there.

Solicitor-general: And the policeman on duty in the hall is downstairs?

Bond: Yes, at the main entrance. No person could come in without passing him.

Solicitor-general: Where does the messenger sit?

Bond: Oh, the reception messenger is there in the room downstairs.

Solicitor-general: He is the messenger who goes down with the letters to the post?

Bond: No, sir; he collects the letters from the Vice-Regal and Chief Secretary's lodges when the Chief Secretary is here.

Solicitor-general: He is often out?

Bond: He is seldom there after eight o'clock.

Chairman: But I suppose any official of the Castle could go in, while the policeman was there, and go up to the telephone without exciting any remark?

Bond: Any known official; but I believe the policeman always accosts them, and he takes mental note of where they are going and sees them in and out. He would know where they were going, and he could always hear them speaking on the telephone.

Solicitor-general: If it is considered desirable it is very easy to ask the policeman, but I believe Mr Harrel can tell us.

Harrel: In the case of Sir Arthur Vicars or any other official going in and out there constantly, the policeman, knowing them so well, would take no notice. It would make no impression on his mind.

Chairman: Then I think there is no use whatever in asking the policeman.

\* \* \* \* \*

Solicitor-general: There is one last matter that I have to mention. You remember that it was stated that two keys of the strong-room were at first supplied?

Chairman: Yes.

Solicitor-general: And two afterwards. It is right to mention that, from the inquiries the police have made, the facts appear to be these. Mr Pemberton was the contractor for the building of the strong-room. He has since died. His son is under the impression, and believes, that the two additional keys, the third and fourth, were supplied to Sir Arthur Vicars through his father, in other words, that it was not Sir Arthur Vicars who applied to the Milner people for them, but that they came to him through Mr Pemberton, the contractor. So it may be taken, I think, that the third and fourth keys came in that way to Sir Arthur Vicars, not as the result of any direct application to the Milner people, but through the contractor.

Starkie: Who paid for them?

Solicitor-general: That I do not know; but it would be a small matter, and for the moment I would not ask the Commission to proceed on the assumption that Sir Arthur Vicars paid for them. I think it is better to take it in that way, as the matter is a little obscure.

Starkie: The Board of Works' witness yesterday stated that they were not paid for by the Board of Works.

Solicitor-general: But the expense was a very trifling matter, and for my part I think at present it would be better to assume that they came to him in the ordinary way, and that they were not the result of any special application or paid for by himself. As the matter is obscure it is better to consider it in that fashion.

The Opinion of the Vice-Regal Commission


Although it was no part of our duty under Your Excellency's Warrant to conduct a criminal investigation into the robbery of the jewels, or to take evidence with a view to the ascertainment of the thief, yet as, on the evidence given before us and now in print, it appears that the name of Mr Francis Richard Shackleton was more than once named as that of the probable or possible author of this great crime, we think it only due to that gentleman to say that he came from San Remo at great inconvenience to give evidence before us, that he appeared to us to be a perfectly truthful and candid witness, and that there was no evidence whatever before us which would support the suggestion that he was the person who stole the jewels.

Having fully investigated all the circumstances connected with the loss of the Regalia of the Order of St Patrick, and having examined and considered carefully the arrangements of the Office of Arms in which the Regalia were deposited, and the provisions made by Sir Arthur Vicars, or under his direction, for their safe keeping, and having regard especially to the inactivity of Sir Arthur Vicars on the occasions immediately preceding the disappearance of the jewels, when he knew that the office and the strongroom had been opened at night by unauthorized persons, we feel bound to report to Your Excellency that, in our opinion, Sir Arthur Vicars did not exercise due vigilance or proper care as the custodian of the Regalia.

We desire to express our obligations to our Secretary, Mr C.T. Beard, of the Chief Secretary's office, for the valuable assistance he gave us in the conduct of our inquiry.

All which we humbly submit for Your Excellency's consideration.

James J. Shaw
Robert F. Starkie
Chester Jones

25 January 1908

*On 30th January 1908 Sir Arthur Vicars' appointment as Ulster King of Arms was terminated. Believing he had been made a scapegoat for the theft of the jewels, he retired, embittered, to County Kerry. He was shot outside his home by a local IRA unit in April 1921.*

*Francis Bennett Goldney died in a motoring accident in France in 1918. His effects were found to include ancient charters and documents belong to the City of Canterbury and other works of art.*

*Pierce Gun Mahony was shot through the heart in 1914 in what appeared to be a hunting accident.*

*Francis Shackleton was convicted of fraud in 1913. He died in Chichester in 1941 under an assumed name.*

*The fate of the Irish Crown Jewels remains a mystery*

**Hansard 27 March 1908**

**Dismissal of Sir Arthur Vicars.**

*House of Commons Debate 27 March 1908 vol 186*

*CAPTAIN CRAIG*

To ask the Chief Secretary to the Lord-Lieutenant of Ireland whether Sir Arthur Vicars' dismissal was decided upon before the 28th October, 1907, and that he was so informed in a letter bearing that date; and, if so, why a Vice-Regal Commission was subsequently appointed to inquire into a matter already judged and decided by the Irish Government.

(Answered by Mr. Birrell.)

On 23rd October, 1907, Sir Arthur Vicars was informed that it had been decided to reconstitute the Office of Arms, and that this would involve his being relieved of the office of Ulster King of Arms. The Vice-Regal Commission was subsequently appointed in consequence of a memorial praying for an inquiry signed by certain Knights of the Order of St. Patrick.

## Moments of History

The British War in Afghanistan
Coastal Command, 1939–1942
Escaping from Germany, 1939–45 (with photos)
Front Line, 1940–1941
The Highland Division by Eric Linklater
The Irish Book of Death and Flying Ships
John Lennon: the FBI files )
Marilyn Monroe: the FBI files
The Mediterranean Fleet: Greece to Tripoli
Sacco and Vanzetti: the FBI files
The Second Afghan War, 1879
The Theft of the Irish Crown Jewels, 1907
Victory in Europe 1945:General Eisenhower's Report
War in Italy

## Uncovered Editions

**Crime**
Rillington Place, 1949
The Strange Story of Adolf Beck
The Trials of Oscar Wilde, 1895

**Ireland**
Bloody Sunday Lord Widgery's Report,1972
The Irish Uprising, 1914–21

**Transport**
The Loss of the Titanic, 1912
R.101: the Airship Disaster, 1930

Tragic Journeys (Titanic, R.101, Munich Air Crash)

**Travel and Empire**
The Amritsar Massacre: General Dyer in the Punjab, 1919
The Boer War: Ladysmith and Mafeking,1900
The British Invasion of Tibet:Colonel Younghusband,1904
Florence Nightingale and the Crimea, 1854–55
King Guezo of Dahomey, 1850–52
Mr Hosie's Journey to Tibet, 1904
The Siege Collection (Kars, Boer War, Peking)
The Siege of Kars, 1855
The Siege of the Peking Embassy, 1900
Travels in Mongolia, 1902
Wilfred Blunt's Egyptian Garden: Fox-hunting in Cairo

**Tudor History**
Letters of Henry VIII, 1526–29

**UK Politics Since 1945**
John Profumo and Christine Keeler, 1963
UFOs in the House of Lords, 1979
War in the Falklands, 1982

**United States of America**
The Assassination of John F. Kennedy, 1963
The Cuban Missile Crisis, 1962
The St Valentine's Day Massacre, 1929
UFOs in America, 1947
The Watergate Affair, 1972

**The War Facsimiles**
(*Illustrated books published by the British government during the war years*)
The Battle of Britain, August–October 1940
The Battle of Egypt, 1942
Bomber Command, September 1939–July 1941
East of Malta,West of Suez,September 1939 to March 1941

Fleet Air Arm, 1943
Land at War, 1939–1944
Ocean Front: the story of the war in the Pacific, 1941–1944
Roof over Britain, 1939–1942

**World War I**
British Battles of World War I, 1914–15
Defeat at Gallipoli:the Dardanelles Commission Part II,1915–16
Lord Kitchener and Winston Churchill:The Dardanelles Commission Part I,1914–15
The Russian Revolution, 1917
War 1914: Punishing the Serbs
The World War I Collection (Dardanelles Commission, British Battles of World War I)

**World War II**
Attack on Pearl Harbor, 1941
D Day to VE Day:General Eisenhower's Report,1944–45
Escape from Germany, 1939–45
The Judgment of Nuremberg, 1946
Tragedy at Bethnal Green
War 1939: Dealing with Adolf Hitler
The World War II Collection (War 1939, D Day to VE Day, Judgment of Nuremberg) *(see also The War Facsimiles)*

Titles can be ordered from
www.amazon.com
www.amazon.co.uk.
www.abebooks.com